THE TAPESTRY OF
OUR LIVES TORN
WITH FEAR

THE TAPESTRY OF OUR LIVES TORN WITH FEAR

✦

LIVING THROUGH THE MCCARTHY WITCH HUNTS

An ugly historical period, family relationships dashed on the sea of double rocks, wounds that will not heal.

A historical Tragedy In an Ugly Historical Period, A Time of Madness.

Clara R. Maslow

iUniverse, Inc.
New York Lincoln Shanghai

THE TAPESTRY OF OUR LIVES TORN WITH FEAR
LIVING THROUGH THE MCCARTHY WITCH HUNTS

iUniverse books may be ordered through booksellers or by contacting:

iUniverse
2021 Pine Lake Road, Suite 100
Lincoln, NE 68512
www.iuniverse.com
1-800-Authors (1-800-288-4677)

ISBN-13: 978-0-595-37328-4 (pbk)
ISBN-13: 978-0-595-81726-9 (ebk)
ISBN-10: 0-595-37328-3 (pbk)
ISBN-10: 0-595-81726-2 (ebk)

Printed in the United States of America

I wish to dedicate this book to my husband, Bernard Maslow:
Thank you for your constant love, for loving me the way
I thought I'd never be loved.

Contents

Bern Maslow was an extraordinary man, a Prince among men, a man Unparalleled,
in intellect wisdom, kindness and generosity, and devotion to his family.
Exceptional in his humanist understanding and compassion for all human beings
and their struggles. He believed in people, and justice for all people. He was an
exceptionally compassionate man, A caring human being.

The early years, growing up with Isaac, his wonderful father. Learning from Isaac.
His love for family, and for people.

The early years at camp; learning Jewish culture.

Memories. Isaac had a dream, to arrange a marriage for us. At the ocean, How we
met and fell in love.

Life before McCarthy was Idyllic as the American Dream. Raising children. Living
in The Vail Homes.

The terribleness of history.

Fear in the crucible of McCarthyism. The witch-hunt and the effects.

psychological effects of terror and fear on our family, our children. Damaged
relationships. Disoriented love.

Disoriented love, relationships on the rocks. Our world gone up in smoke.
Damaged relationships into the third generation.

ACKNOWLEDGMENTS

For special encouragement and support and help I wish to thank my loving son, Jonathan Maslow, and my special love granddaughter Emily Rachel Cohen, who have kept me living to produce this work. I am grateful to Dan Englander, a talented young man who helped put all of this on the computer. And, to Sharon Rudnitzky, for the lovely photograph on the cover.

PREFACE

Senator Joe McCarthy and legislative Aide Roy Cohn at U.S.Army
McCarthy Hearings, 1954

"As John and Elizabeth struggle to maintain their sanity, and integrity in a world gone mad, their faces whether frightened or angry, or lost, become an illuminated index of the utter madness and savagery of the human beings around them."

—Arthur Miller, The Crucible, 1953

1

Arthur Miller's award winning play The Crucible is a story of people's individual conscience and the social tyranny achieved by a small group who were whipped up with terror and fear by a few ambitious leaders. "The result of popular hysterical fear of the Devil." The narrative is about a cry of protest by the innocent victims against the tyranny of a few leaders. The story takes place in the small village of Salem, Mass., in 1692, when nineteen men and women and two dogs were hanged for witchcraft. For Miller, past events and present realities are pressed together by a moral logic. This is a constant theme in all of his works. In The Crucible, Miller intends to create an analogy with the McCarthyism of the 1950's; with the red-baiting and the communist witch hunts and inquisition of the House Un-American Activities Committee as part of the Truman Administration's anti-communist crusade. The McCarthy witch hunts succeeded in instituting a reign of terror among the population. It created a climate of fear among the American people against the (hypothetical) hunt for "communists and spies" working for the government. It was an allegory of our times. It was a time of utter madness.

"The question is not the reality of witches, but the power of authority (the state) to define the nature of the real," wrote Miller. The Crucible is a play about the nature of power. It is an intense psychological drama about an entire community betrayed by a Dionysian surrender to the irrational, that is driven by a cultivation of fear" It is" Greek tragedy" at its finest.
Miller makes the connection superbly; "It is an allegory of our times." "Gradually over weeks, a living connection between Salem and Washington, was made in my mind—I saw that the hearings (U.S. Army-McCarthy Hearings 1954), were profoundly and avowedly ritualistic." "The same spiritual nugget lay folded within both procedures." The political realities of the early 1950's presented problems for those who became the innocent victims (like the innocent victims in the Salem Witch Trials). It is in this climate of fear, an ugly historical period the McCarthy witch hunts, that this memoir takes place.

In America it was the heart of darkness, the worst of times, a time of horrendous historical nightmare. The 1950's was unequivocally an ugly period of America's history. It was the time of the build up of the Cold War when the Truman Administration was using "red squads" and red-baiting, to scare and frighten the American people against the communism of the Soviet Union. It was the time when J. Edgar Hoover, head of the FBI, presided over the huge anti-communist crusade. A time of Loyalty Oaths for government employees, a time of blacklisting of The Hollywood Ten. It was the time of the House Un-American Committee (HUAC) investigations—the inquisitions held by the unabashedly war-mongering Senator Pat McCarran and his ominous bill known as the 1950 Internal Security Act, known as The McCarran Act. This later became known as "the direct threat to liberty in America since the Alien and Sedition Acts of 1798." McCarran was known as one of the most virulent redbaiters of the age. He shepherded major anti-communist laws through Congress. Known as a dyspeptic, power-hungry titan—driven by hatreds and resentments (and bigotry), he drove the nation's legislative agenda. He conducted gratuitous persecutions, waged in the name of the hunt for spies. He helped create the climate of fear, instituted by a few politicians in power against the entire nation.

Senator Joe McCarthy at U.S. Army McCarthy Hearings, 1954

Miller said, "We were all going slightly crazy, trying to be safe. The hysteria in Salem had a certain inner procedure which we were duplicating once again."

In the U.S. it was a time when "Hell was spreading all over the world like a drop of ink on blotting paper." It was a time when, a year before the U.S. Army McCarthy hearings began, J. Edgar Hoover sent the FBI to every neighborhood to interrogate all the neighbors, including the Vail Homes, the government housing project where we were living, along with most of the engineers and their families. They wanted to know, "What do they read? What kind of literature is in their garbage? Who are their friends?" Who are their relatives?" "What organizations do they belong to?"

This memoir is the story of our family, Bern and I and our two young children, who were victims of the McCarthy witch hunts, in the U.S. Army McCarthy Hearings of 1954.

This is the memoir of Bernard Maslow, a remarkable man, a man unparalleled in intellectual ability, in wisdom and humaneness, an exceptionally devoted husband and father, and a victim of the horrendous McCarthy witch hunt held at Ft. Monmouth, N.J. It is the personal story of the effects of trauma we suffered in the McCarthy witch hunts, our own personal struggle to overcome the fear and paranoia instituted by the government and McCarthy over the population at the time, and the long term effects on our two beautiful and bright children in terms of damaged personal relationships. And now into the third generation—with our granddaughter, who has had her share of problems with her mother (our daughter) in growing up.

This was the time of the House Un-American Activities Committee (HUAC), and the passage of Truman's Loyalty Oath for civilians working for the government. And, it was the time of the Congressional Hearings with J.Parnell Thomas as Speaker of the House interrogating those suspected of being communists. The Hollywood Ten were the most prominent witnesses. Most of the writers and directors who were accused lost their jobs and their careers.. For them, it was destroying their work, and in most cases their families as well (see "I'd Hate Myself in The Morning," by Ring Lardner Jr. 2000)

In 1954, Bern was working as engineer, Assistant Director of the Photographic Research Labs, at the Army Signal Corps Engineering Laboratories at Ft.Monmouth, N.J. We were a happy young loving couple with two extraordinarily beautiful and bright children, Jane, 9, and Jonathan, 6. Bern loved his work, he loved being an engineer, and he loved working for the government, where he was able to use his exceptional intellectual and mathematical skills, as well as his wonderful humanism as an administrator. He was loved and respected by everyone., both the civilian engineers, and especially the military personnel with whom he worked closely.

He had served in the US Navy, for three years, and now he was able to work and provide for his family, his first love. Bern was passionately in love with his family, with me and our children with an unparalleled devotion and commitment to take care of us, and to provide for us. Our life was our family. We were living the American Dream in a landscape of sheer love and devotion and work striving to give meaning to our lives and for our children.

In March 1954, Senator Joseph McCarthy the infamous "Tail-Gunner," marched into The Research Labs at Ft. Monmouth. Like molten lava spreading out from a burning volcano, he came to hold the U.S. Army McCarthy Hearings. He was accompanied by his two malevolent aides David Shine and Roy Cohn, on the red baiting rampage of the administration's war against communism. There had previously been 160 closed hearings held during this campaign in preparation for this public hearing. The hearing was televised daily throughout the region and across the nation for weeks.

Every day one could see Joe McCarthy's menacing face leering into the camera, frothing and lunging while holding up a ream of papers, claiming, "I have here a list of 250 names of communists and spies working for the government." "These men are traitors, disloyal to their country. They must be routed out, sent to prison for life." As it turned out, no spy was ever found, no one was ever convicted of spying.

Dalton Trumbo was the most famous of the Hollywood Ten writers who was hauled before the HUAC Committee, accused of being a "communist spy". He wrote amazing letters about life under the Hollywood Blacklist. These letters and other documents, sealed by the government, were released in 2001. In Trumbo's words, "Those too young to remember the McCarthy era should not waste time searching for "villains or heroes or saints or devils, because there were none. There were only victims."

By coincidence, the Senate Committee on Governmental Affairs has released five volumes of secret testimony from the closed hearings held during McCarthy's red baiting rampage, during the 1954–1957 years. (He died in 1957) Along with the Dalton Trumbo letters and other memoirs, these documents are particularly timely and relevant in today's political climate. It emphasizes once again the apparent failure of our political culture to grasp the distinction between dissent and disloyalty. Instead they rely on creating a state of fear in the nation in order to control the people. It is as true today as it was then, as it was in1692, the time of the Salem witch trials.

Joe McCarthy arrived at Ft. Monmouth in the Spring of 1954. Almost immediately, Bern received notice from his administrator that he was being removed from his job. He was removed as Assistant Director of the Photo Research Labs, and sent to an empty barracks building at the far end of Ft. Monmouth. His security clearance was removed, making him unemployable. At the time most corporations were working on government contracts and all their employees were required to have security clearance. We were never told why he was suspended. He remained in this state of limbo, no job, no work for three years.

We were thrown into a state of absolute terror, fear and panic. Bern experienced total shock at losing his job and security clearance. It was an inconceivable catastrophe happening to this wonderful man, husband and father. It was as if he was being enveloped in a burning volcano. The fact that he could not get a job because of the loss of his security clearance was at least as frightening to him as the fear and panic created by losing his job. He did not know what would happen to him or to us. He was devastated at the thought that he would not be able to provide for his family. And he was worried. He could not imagine that the government, his employer, would allow this to happen to such loyal employees.

A tidal wave of terror and fear swept over our family, and over the entire community. As if we were suddenly drowning under a great river's raging current, twisting and turning as we struggled to find our way to the surface to get our bearings. It all happened so fast we did not have time to question, to understand, although we knew the seriousness of what was happening. The blow to beloved Bern was indescribable, overwhelming violence to his self esteem. Dashed was his image of devoted husband and father, caretaker and provider for his family. We were in a state of shock, close to envying the dead. Bern was fearful that he would not make a living and provide for his loved ones. We were living through an epic historical tragedy, the tragedy of McCarthyism that became a public nightmare. It was a climate of fear and terror, imposed by the McCarthy witch hunts, and Loyalty Oath and red baiting of the Truman Administration. We were the innocent victims, reflecting the utter madness and savagery of the perpetrators around us.

Everyday I opened the TV to watch the Army-McCarthy Hearing, only to see the menacing, leering, lurching face of Joe McCarthy. I found myself crying, sobbing all day for my beloved Bern. When our two young children came home from school and found me crying, as I watched the hearing unfold, they hugged me and cried with me. They were too young to understand the meaning, but they understood and felt the deep emotional crisis we were experiencing, and they internalized the fear, and terror we were feeling. The horrible experience of McCarthy had torn our lives apart and we did not know what the consequences would be. We were in a state of complete and utter shock. The fear was palpable. Fear pervaded our life completely.

The terror and fear created by McCarthy's witch hunt hearing on TV had spread throughout the civilian population of Ft. Monmouth and the surrounding communities. It had also spread throughout the nation. It was on the TV news all day and night. People were frozen with fear. No one called on the phone, we were afraid because we knew the phones were being tapped. We lived in this state of frozen fear for months without communicating. It was a time of utter darkness, and we were caught in the true heart of darkness. The stark images of this paralyzing fear are still with me. "It feels like something out of a Hieronomous Bosch painting of hell." I can still feel it in my bones. And I know that my beloved Bern lived with this persistent fear all his life. The paranoia persisted, as Victor Navasky said, "Although most illusions about communism of the Cold War may be exhausted, the paranoia left over from those years persists."

Bern was normally a pillar of strength, a man of wisdom and confidence, now he was disheartened, a man beaten down by the fear and paranoia which had penetrated his psyche. He slept very little, he was nervous and jumpy, and fearful, his temper became like a short fuse. For the rest of his life he fretted and worried about us, our safety and our health.. He wanted to protect us, to care for us. And he was fearful that something would arise from the dead to prevent it.

It is said that terrorism provides the best soil-culture for panic, fear and paranoia. We were caught in the crucible of McCarthyism. We were trapped in the witch hunt Army-McCarthy hearing, supposedly in the name of the Cold War hunt for communists and spies in the government. McCarthy had created a reign of terror, panic and fear over the land for political ends. And we were among the innocent victims. We were reflecting the utter madness and savagery of the perpetrators around us. As Miller had said.

The purpose of instituting a reign of terror and fear was in order to muffle dissent. The Truman administration was embarked on a huge military build up under the umbrella of fighting communism. They wanted to discourage dissent. The victims of terrorism tend to become demoralized. The effect is incomprehensible and "nightmarish". The victims of this type of psychological violence also may become dysfunctional. That is what happened in our case. After the initial terror and panic subsided, after the children were able to accommodate to the initial blow, they each developed their own form of dysfunctional relationship with us. When Jane was a young adolescent, when Jonathan was in late adolescence, each developed their own obsessive neurosis. The normal wires of our close loving relationship became twisted, taking an ugly turn. Love became disoriented. Eventually, the dysfunctional relationship was passed on to our granddaughter,

As a political instrument, psychological terrorism and violence "destroys the ends for which it is employed, killing the user as well as his victim. It has become the path to hell on earth, and the end of the earth." (Jonathan Schell, The Nation, 2002) Violence is a mark of human failure and it brings only sorrow. Sorrow and fear became the woven tapestry of our lives. We wore its mantle the rest of our lives.

For the next three years, while Bern spent everyday at the empty barracks at Fort Monmouth, our lives were driven by his fear and his wish to escape from this horrendous nightmare. With his inherent wisdom he realized that he must start a private business to make a living for his family. He did not trust the government or the security of a government job. He had been betrayed and victimized. And he did not want his family to suffer. He put all his time and effort into planning a business, which would provide a living for us, and would not depend on a security clearance from the government.

At the end of three years Bern had succeeded in putting together the plans to build a bowling alley; the plans to buy the property, the plans for the construction of the building and the equipment, and the financing and the managing. He also put together a group of investors for the financing. The investors were two businessmen, a real estate developer and a lawyer. Bern would manage the entire project from beginning to end. His plans were complete, The investors were very happy with Bern's financial projection of a good profit. The project was successful. And, after Bern was returned to his job at the Signal Corps, he continued to manage the construction and completion and managing of the bowling alley. At that time, he was working two jobs. Later, he took on another job.

"But McCarthyism bequeathed America much more, as Ellen Schrecker wrote in "McCarthyism in America." It changed the lives of thousands of people at the same time that it changed the nation's political culture. The anti communist crusade was complex and touched so many aspects of American life. There was a lot of human wreckage…The anti communist crusade blighted thousands of lives, careers, and marriages…Some were destroyed. All experienced stress. Genuine innocents had the worst time."

"Life in America had changed". But beyond the lives and careers of the men and women directly caught up in it there has been no systematic attempt to catalogue those effects or assess their long term influence. "Much of the damage that McCarthyism imposed was psychological. For an entire generation of law-abiding men and women it was devastating. The lawyers who worked with these people invariably talked about their trauma and other emotional problems. And the affect on their families. "They would just go to pieces." (Schrecker)

Moreover, the McCarthy anti-communist crusade interfered with the ongoing work of the federal agencies that came under attack. By the time McCarthy had finished interrogating the engineers at the U.S. Army's Signal Corps Labs, at Ft. Monmouth, the facility's ongoing research was disrupted, and the morale of the remaining engineers was undermined. Within a year, many of the top professionals had quit. A panel of expert scientists in 1955, warned that "unless the installation's personnel problems were corrected the laboratories might be incapable of carrying out their assigned missions."

Many assumed that McCarthyism died with the death of Joe McCarthy (1957) and that the ravaging of innocent American citizens had stopped. But he was riding a tide that continued to resume and to swell throughout the decades of the

Cold War. In every profession, from teachers, to salesmen, to linotypes, union leaders and librarians, individuals continued to be fired.

Today we are once again confronted with proving "patriotism." The "War on Terrorism" is the new jihad, the new McCarthyism in the similarities in creating a climate of terrorism and fear. (Eric Foner, Professor of History, Columbia University)

The analogy to McCarthyism, at present, is the self appointed guardians who are engaging in private black-listing, trying to intimidate individuals with a different point of view. There aren't loyalty oaths being demanded of teachers—yet. But we seem to be at the beginning of a process that could get a lot worse and is already cause for considerable alarm. (Eric Foner, The Progressive, 02)

At end of the 19th century, Joseph Conrad, wrote Heart of Darkness. He understood that the distinctions between civilized society and the heart of darkness quickly collapsed in extreme situations. And could fall into the most barbarous practices against its own citizens. Bern and our family lived through the most savage period of McCarthyism, the pit of heart of darkness.

Bern's experience, our family experience as victims of the McCarthy reign of terror and fear, and the witch hunt of the Ft. Monmouth hearing with its devastating effects on our family relationships, must be chronicled. It must be reported and written down for history. And as a narrative of human tragedy, and the evil that men can do.

I want this memoir to be remembered. I want it to be remembered that this happened here in America to our loving family. That it happened to innocent civilian employees. That the effect of McCarthy's barbarous political, demagogic tactics caused the emotional upheaval in our family that resulted in the dysfunctional personal relationships between us and between the children themselves; and into the third generation. That this madness that occurred must not be allowed to happen again. We have to do everything we can to make sure that it never happens again. We must not allow the rise of a demagogue, or the creation by the state of a reign of terror and fear and repression that devastates the lives of innocent Americans. Psychological terrorism is killing to the emotional lives of the people caught in its net. It has long lasting and damaging effects on its victims. Our experience with the nightmarish event of McCarthyism and psychological terrorism and fear is still palpable in our lives. The fear lingers on.

The story of my husband Bern Maslow, and our family caught in the crucible of McCarthyism, in the U.S. Army-McCarthy hearings (1954), is a historical memoir. A tapestry torn by the historical force turned to personal nightmare.

"We must not only seek but find an alternative, because the world offered to us is unbearable. For years simply to seek a new world has been either a crime or a folly. From now on, it is the main item on the agenda." (Daniel Singer, 2000)

1

REMEMBERING BERN MASLOW, AN EXTRAORDINARY MAN

"At rare intervals there appears among us a man of such extraordinary qualities and sensibilities combining profound intellect and wisdom, and selfless devotion and generosity of spirit, who has such a capacity for love of people, for relating to every sort of human being, who subordinates his own ego needs in the concern of others, and whose virtues are manifest to all that he is loved and revered by everyone with whom he comes in contact." (Ring Lardner Jr., 2000)

My husband Bern Maslow was an extraordinary man, a wonderful man, a man unparalleled as a human being in wisdom, intellect and caring and devotion to his family, and to every human being who knew him. Bern was an exceptional man not only for his own family but for everyone who ever worked with him. Early in our married life, when our children were young Bern became a victim of the anti-communist crusade initiated by the Truman Administration to carry on the Cold War, and primarily by Senator Joseph McCarthy who personally and with the support of the administration conducted the witch hunt for "spies and communists" working for the government. In particular, the witch-hunt of the U.S. Army McCarthy Hearing, 1954 held at Ft. Monmouth, N.J. where Bern was employed as a civilian engineer. We were innocent victims of the reign of terror, and fear created by McCarthy in his insidious hunt for "communists' working for the government. We managed to live through the horrible climate of terror and fear instituted at the time. Only to find that the traumatic effects of this horrible experience to our family, caught in the crucible of McCarthyism severely damaged our personal family relationships for years to come; And into the third generation with our granddaughter.

It was the 1950's, the early years of the Cold War initiated by the Truman administration as the war on communism. It was the height of activities of McCarthyism and the reign of terror he instituted. It was the ugly period of Joe McCarthy and his witch-hunts and the US. Army McCarthy Hearings, and the irrevocable damage that McCarthyism did to so many honest American citizens. McCarthyism has become a metaphor for "witch hunt", for the search for "spies", or "disloyal" workers, and for creating the climate of "terror, as an intense overwhelming fear" in order to convince and coerce the American people in its crusade against the USSR as the enemy. It is the use of terror and fear and repressive measures by the government to coerce the citizens into a state that can be harmful to their lives. This memoir draws the line of connection between the political landscape, the crusade against (the USSR) and climate of terror and fear instituted by the government itself and the real historical events (McCarthyism) that followed, and the character and psychology of its victims. It demonstrates the power of the government's endorsement of the mind-set of terrorism and fear that can create long-lasting psychological damage for its victims.

What is significant about this memoir and the story of our lives which were so damaged, so disoriented and affected so adversely by the McCarthy witch hunts, and the hysteria which dominated the political/social culture of the 1950's is its contemporary resonance. The same climate of terrorism and fear is being enacted (or re-enacted) today by the present administration in their "war on terrorism" and passage of The Patriot Act. To many historians writing today this is a repetition, a McCarthy Redux. We must be active, we must be watchful, we must do everything we can to stop this madness. (Howard Zinn. Professor of History)

For Bern, whose life meant devotion and caring, for his loved ones, and for those who worked with him, and those in need, he subordinated his own needs for consideration of others. Quite simply, he was not like other men. He was a man unparalleled, a prince among men.

Bern Maslow, an Extraordinary Man: Isaac, an Exceptional Father

It is said that the child must be father to the man. Bern as a very young child was raised in the image of his wonderful father Isaac, with all his exceptional qualities of love and caring. He was in every way, every part of his character like Isaac; physically, with the same strong handsome face, the same strong build, white hair and deep set sparkling sapphire blue eyes. Like Isaac he had the same keen intelligence, and sensitivity, warmth and caring. He had feelings of compassion for all human beings. Bern was bonded strongly to Isaac as a little boy. He loved his father deeply, with all his soul.

Bern was a quiet man, a gentle, soft-spoken man, like gentle Isaac. He had the same rare qualities, of caring and passionate love of family, and as well, generosity and concern for people. He was warm, affectionate, gentle and giving. When we first met, by the arrangement of loving Isaac, I was struck by his face. He looked exactly like Isaac, a rugged handsome persona, so sensitive, so gentle, such deep-set sparkling sapphire blue eyes. So knowing, with such integrity such grace that it evoked reverence in me. A rare individual, chosen for me, to take care of me, by his father Isaac.

Bern was a rare individual. He was intellectually gifted, thoughtful, generous and kind. Along with a gifted mind he had a generous spirit. This is described by Nietzche, "very rare among men." As a young man, under the guidance and mentoring of Isaac, he was always seeking knowledge, probing and analyzing the current issues, as a filter for his own experiences. He always strove to act intelligently and responsibly. As Camus wrote, "The problem is to acquire the knowledge of life that goes beyond the ordinary, the mundane." Bern's inner landscape of deep consciousness and responsibility compelled him to seek out the life experiences appropriate to his inner gifts. He was erudite and profoundly thoughtful. He loved people.

As a little boy, bonding with Isaac, Bern developed his superior intellect, his political ideology, and his warmth and love of people. He also learned his interest in people especially the values of social justice, and the conditions that affect people adversely and cause injustice and inequality. He learned his intense warmth and love for family, and his compassion for others. Isaac was Bern's idol and mentor. Bern was exactly like Isaac.

Bern was an exceptional little boy, he was born with musical talent. He had a musical ear and loved to listen to music. He began to play the piano at age 5. His mother took him for piano lessons to the Neighborhood Playhouse, in Brooklyn, where they lived. This was a School For The Arts, and a cultural center for children, where they learned music, dance and painting. Bern took piano lessons. The music teacher marked on his certificate that he was "a gifted young musician." She described his piano playing, "A musical lad with fine feeling for tonal contrasts. His finger training is as yet inadequate, his wrists stiff, but he has so much natural musical feeling that he expresses his intentions effectively notwithstanding. With careful direction along pianistic lines he should accomplish much." (New York Music Week Association, March 21, 1925.)

With his highly gifted musical ear, and love of music, all his life Bern loved and listened to classical music. He especially loved the opera and at an early age he began listening to the broadcasts of the New York Metropolitan Opera Company every Saturday afternoon on the radio. He knew every opera, every libretto, every aria. He followed his favorite opera stars. He taped all his favorites, and favorite singers. His collection of tapes of operas sits on the shelf of his bookcase. He played them frequently while he was working on other things.

Bern also loved symphony music. When he was an adolescent in high school he used to listen faithfully every Sunday afternoon to the N.Y. Philharmonic Symphony Orchestra broadcast on the radio. He had memorized every score of every symphony. He knew all the music, as well as the artists and the conductors. The piano was always his favorite. He loved the piano concertos. He taped all his favorites. He always played his records while he was working.

In the mid-1970's, after we moved to Concord, Mass., Bern soon searched out classical musical concerts that were available in the Boston center. He found the Handel and Haydn Society and its concert series, and subscribed to the concert series, which we attended for the next ten years. He especially loved the choral singing of Handel's Messiah. He had a wonderful appreciation of all the arts. As a child he had attended some classes of Modern Dance at the Brooklyn Neighborhood Playhouse, but his real love was for the ballet. When the children were young, Bern always watched for the performances of the NYC Ballet, and made sure that he got tickets for us to attend. He wanted to make sure that we had the same opportunities to develop his love of culture and the arts. This was the legacy of his father Isaac that he was committed to give to his children.

Bern continued to say, all his life, that the happiest years of his life were spent at summer camp. When he was 7, his parents Isaac and Lisa sent him to Camp Kinderland, a children's camp located north of New York City, in the Finger Lakes Region of upper New York State. Camp Kinderland was founded in 1923 as a summer camp by a group of secular Jews who were active in the trade union movements in New York City. Many of the workers in the trade unions wanted a children's summer camp for their children who were growing up in the city. They wanted a child-centered, culturally oriented, rich environment for their children. The camp was managed by trained professionals, teachers, social workers, and college students as counselors. The program provided the best cultural and intellectual environment and experiences for the development of the children physically, intellectually, educationally and socially. The training in sports included group sports, as well as individual sports such as swimming, canoeing, tennis. Bern became a skilled sportsman, he excelled in tennis and canoeing. He played tennis all his life, two and three times a week. And he taught many younger men to play and to enjoy the sport. And there were lectures and group discussions galore. For the children it was the most intellectually stimulating environment possible. And as well it was great fun.

Bern was a quiet, thoughtful young boy, he was not shy but was not overly outgoing. Bern was only 7 when his parents sent him to Camp Kinderland, He attended Kinderland every summer until he outgrew the camper's age, about seventeen.
Kinderland is the Yiddish word for "children's world". The camp environment represented a melding of Yiddish culture, literature and history, with Jewish humor, intellectual training and healthy living. The camp activities included reading the best Jewish literature, including Sholem Aleichem, the most famous Jewish author. There were daily discussions, and weekly lectures by prominent teachers, professors, and authors. The founders of the camp were mostly progressive people. In camp Bern lived and played with young people from a similar cultural background that he was raised in, they were his intellectual peers, and with whom he became life long friends. In this warm stimulating environment Bern developed his very own gifted qualities and talents into the wonderful extraordinary man that he was.

When Bern was a young boy, 6 or 7 years, he was prone to ear infections. Today, many young children have ear infections which are successfully treated with antibiotics, As a result they are able to fight off the infections but do not remain with scars that leave them handicapped. The use of antibiotics does not injure the delicate mechanism of the middle ear. But in Bern's time, the years of the 20's and 30's, antibiotics were not yet available. In Bern's case, every time he developed an ear infection, the doctor would puncture the thin drum membrane to allow it to drain. The result was that these punctures developed scar tissue which prevented the drum from oscillating properly. Bern developed many infections, in both ears and as a result, both ear drums developed scar tissue. This meant that the ear drums could not vibrate properly. This scarring left Bern with a hearing loss in both ears; as much as 40% to 50% in each ear. Bern grew up as a hearing handicapped child. He wore a hearing aid in the better ear for many years all through high school and college. The hearing handicap remained until after he left the Navy service. By then there was new medical technology to assist and restore the vibration of the ear drums. After he left the service he had the newly developed ear operation to remove the ear-drum, and replace it with a stint that permits vibration. His hearing was restored in both ears using this technology. He had normal hearing in both ears until later in his life, in his seventies, he began to lose the hearing in one ear.

Bern was intellectually gifted and he was musically talented. In elementary school the teachers recognized his superior intelligence, he skipped grades several times. Thus by age 15 he had finished the high school curriculum. He went on to City College (CCNY) to study mechanical engineering. By age 19, he had finished a master's degree in mechanical engineering. He went to work as a mechanical engineer at age 20, for a private firm in NYC, which made locks for suitcases and briefcases. From there he went to work as engineer for the Civil Service Commission, in NYC.

Bern was an exceptional man. He had a keen intellect, a generosity of spirit, a passionate love for family. Bern was a gentle man, a quiet man, soft spoken, with strong beliefs, gathered over time along side his exceptional father Isaac. He lived his life to take care of us in the image of wonderful Isaac.

With his exceptional wisdom, Bern realized that as he was growing up with his handicap (bilateral hearing loss), that if he wanted to provide security for a wife and children he needed to be in a job that was secure, like the government service, instead of working for a corporation, where there was little or no security. With careful forethought he took the Civil Service exam for Mechanical Engineer. He made a perfect score, and got a job right away with the U.S. Civil Service Commission. He was assigned to personnel in charge of hiring engineers for the government. It was the beginning of the World War II build up. As the War heated up the government needed more civilian engineers. Bern was transferred to Ft. Monmouth, N.J. home of the U.S. Army Signal Corps. He was in Personnel, in charge of hiring all civilian engineers. After the War ended he was made Asst. Director Photographic Research Labs. The Signal Corps at Ft.

Monmouth was responsible for communications research for the military. We met just months before he was transferred to Ft. Monmouth. It was fortunate that I was living and worked near Ft. Monmouth in Red Bank, N.J. where I was a Social Worker for the state. (State of N.J. Aid to Dependent Children). We met at a pre-arranged meeting, as if ordained. It was arranged by Isaac, Bern's wonderful father.

2

REMEMBERING ISAAC

Bernard Maslow putting promotion bars on Military Officer, Signal
Corps, Ft. Monmouth, 1953

Of Isaac: I was struck by his wide open wonderful face, so gentle, so sensitive, so kind, with sparkling blue eyes reflecting such obvious reverence that one must admire and love him almost immediately. Quite simply, he was not like other men. Isaac was an exceptional man.

Isaac was not like other men, he was extraordinary, with his keen intellect, his superb wisdom, his concern for his family, and for other people who were less fortunate. His love for children was especially notable. Isaac's warm kind loving nature and his love for children made him a modern day Pied Piper. The children recognized his warm loving qualities, they automatically felt his love for them. Isaac and Bern were very much alike, as if in the image of each other, sharing the same qualities, the same generosity, the same sensibilities, the same thinking, the same beliefs. Both had a similar understanding of the world; the politics, the economy, the institutions, the systems, the real world, and both had the same love of human beings. Each was a Prince of men, in his own right.

"Life gained meaning in the service of a cause" in the words of Max Weber, German writer and critic. He wrote "Politics brought direction to the frantic stasis of life." Weber wrote about the world of the working class, mostly "of immigrant Jews and disenfranchised workers" who were generally seated around the kitchen table in their apartments arguing politics late into the night. These people were eventually transformed into the nation's "thinkers, writers, lawyers, poets, the makers of the world." This is the culture in which Isaac lived. Bern learned from Isaac to be an intellectual, a gifted social thinker. And to live his life, like Isaac, for his family, his children, and his country. Both Isaac and Bern were passionate about the issues of social justice and equality: "a beautiful vision, but instead he was devastated and in despair by the world's failure to live up to its own vision." For both Isaac and Bern, this represented the core of their ideology. Both were committed to making the world a better place not only for their own children, but for all people, all children. This was their raison d'etre, their contribution, their striving to give value and meaning to their lives.

Isaac came to the U.S. as a young boy in the early 1900's, as an immigrant from Eastern Russia, in the Ukraine region. It was the horrendous time of the Czar with his repressive barbarous pogroms against the Jews. It was a time of police killings and terrorizing of ordinary citizens. The population lived in utter fear, especially the Jews, who were the most persecuted. Like many young men from Jewish families, Isaac was well educated. Like many other young Jewish intellectuals he was being harassed by the local police—the gendarmes. As a young man, when he first started to work he had been a member of the Jewish Labor Bund. And as an activist for the Labor Union he was involved in operating an illegal press to disseminate and distribute the pamphlets and other materials to the working population. This was the time of the beginning of unionization of the working people under the Russian dictatorship of the Czar. It was a time of extreme repression by the police. The police of course assumed that the work Isaac was doing—operating a press, was subversive. It was illegal and therefore must be punished. The police were sent to investigate him. That was when he decided it was time to leave the country. He immigrated to America.

Isaac arrived and settled in Philadelphia where he had friends. There he met Lisa Baskin, a handsome young woman living with her family. One brother, Samuel, was a Rabbi, the other brother, Louis, lived with his wife in Los Angeles. Lisa was working in a shop in the garment industry as an expert seamstress on ladies' blouses. Soon Isaac and Lisa were married in Philadelphia where both their children, Sophie and Bern, were born.

When the children were young, the family moved to Brooklyn where Isaac had established a business. With a partner he had opened a dental laboratory, making dental appliances for dentists, like crowns, false teeth, bridges, etc. The business was successful for many years, Both families made a good living, They were able to send their children to camp and to college. Today, the son of the (original) partner is still operating the dental lab in the same location in Brooklyn.

Isaac was exceptionally gentle and kind, a loving man. Isaac never met a child that he did not drape with a fuzzy bear hug. He knew many friends who had young children who were overjoyed when he came to visit. He had enormous love and compassion, and empathy. Bern inherited these qualities of love for children and love and compassion for all human beings. Bern was a most affectionate husband and father, like Isaac. He was most compassionate and sympathetic to everyone he worked with, like Isaac. And, he was a wonderful giving human being, like Isaac. And, with Isaac as mentor, he developed his own philosophy and perspective of life in the service of a utopian cause and vision. Life meant to take care of all those who needed him.

Albert Camus said, "the problem of evil is the fundamental intellectual question of the world. In the development of one's political ideology, the development of the self, life gained meaning in the service of a cause. The disciplined activist is not a utopian inspired by a beautiful vision, but devastated by the world's failure to live up to his vision."

3

THE TERRIBLENESS OF HISTORY: WOUNDS THAT WILL NOT HEAL

Petronila, a Mayan woman doesn't know how old she is but she knows very well how long it has been since her life was shattered in the Guatemalan War—nineteen years. "I want it to be remembered that this happened now. Here. We have to do everything to make sure that this never happens again," she says. "I don't hate anyone, maybe they were forced to do it. But when I see soldiers, I am still afraid. I know what people like that did to my family, they raped and killed. This must never happen again in our country."

This memoir is to commemorate Bern Maslow, an extraordinary man, an exceptional devoted husband and father, a man unparalleled in wisdom, intellect, human kindness and generosity, remarkable for his humanity, his generosity of spirit who stood out as a beacon. His concern for the human struggle, for a humane and just society for all served as an icon. He was a rare human being, passionately in love with his family, compassionate for all. He was a Prince among men.

Bern Maslow and our family were victims caught in the crucible of McCarthyism. From a loving family with two beautiful and bright children we became victims of the reign of terror and fear instituted by the invidious McCarthy, and the Truman administration, in the U.S. Army McCarthy witch hunt hearing, at Ft. Monmouth New Jersey in 1954. It was the trumped up cause of hunting for "spies and communists" working in the government. Our family life was damaged irrevocably for years, for the rest of our lives. This must never again happen in our country.

It was the best of times, it was the worst of times. It was after the war, World War II, against Hitler and the Nazis in Germany, and the fascists in Italy. Bern had served in the U.S. Navy as engineer at the U.S. Naval Depot, Newport, Va., for three years.

It was the best of times for us, as Bern had come home from service to resume his job as civilian engineer for the Signal Corps at Ft. Monmouth. He was made Asst. Director, Photographic Research Laboratory. There were over 400 civilian engineers working at the research labs on communication research for the military services.

It was the best of times, it was the happiest of times for us. We had two beautiful bright young children, Jane and Jonathan. We were fortunate to live at The Vail Homes which was a government-built housing project, built for the civilian engineers and service personnel, and their families. It was located in Eatontown, N.J., next to Ft. Monmouth, but separated from the town. The Vail Homes was a unique community of mostly young, happy people working in jobs they loved, for the government, and raising their children in a wonderful community in an atmosphere of camaraderie, congeniality and kindness. It was a most happy place for raising children, they had the best of times.

For us it was the best of times, that turned into the worst of times. It turned into a nightmare, a heart of darkness for us, a time of bleakness, darkness and despair, as it became for many other innocent Americans working for the government. It was in the 50's, the time of the Truman Administration, the crusade of the Cold War, and most importantly, the time of McCarthyism. It was the time of Truman's Loyalty Oath, the time of the HUAC Committee, time of the Hollywood Ten, and the McCarran Act, and the persecution and hunt for "communists and spies" working for the government. But worst of all, it was the time of Joe McCarthy and his witch hunts for supposed "spies" and "communists". A time when the FBI under J.Edgar Hoover prosecuted many people, mostly innocent American citizens. A time of national convulsion, familiar now only to those who were exposed to the spectacle of Joseph McCarthy frothing at the mouth and lunging into the TV in the U.S. Army McCarthy Hearings, at Ft. Monmouth, N.J. The malice in his face was unforgettable. And the malevolence and ugliness in the faces of his aides, Roy Cohn and David Shine, was unforgettably disheartening.

Suddenly, in Spring 1954, it was as if the sky was suddenly blackened by Black Hawk helicopters. Joe McCarthy, and his two aides (Roy Cohn and David Shine) descended on Ft. Monmouth with hundreds of television camera crews to the Military Trial Court, to hold the "U.S. Army McCarthy Hearing", a witch hunt in the true style of the Salem Witch Trials. The stated purpose was to route out "communists and spies" working for the government, (at the Signal Corps, Ft. Monmouth). The hearing was televised daily. Senator McCarthy appeared on the screen daily, lunging and frothing, holding up a batch of papers, screaming, "I have here a list of 250 names of communists and spies working for the government. These men are traitors, they must be routed out, punished. They must be sentenced to prison for life." "We must make our country safe."

That same day, inside the Labs, Bern, (along with about 50 other engineers), was quietly and swiftly removed from his job, and his security clearance was removed. These men were sent to an empty barracks at the far end of the base, without a word of explanation. It was as if they were sent to purgatory to await punishment. There was no explanation given. They were never told why they had been fired, or how long they would remain in limbo. They were treated as criminals—declared guilty before tried in the eyes of the world.

Bern came home that day, he was white as a sheet. He could hardly speak. He looked as if he had been given a death sentence. We were in a state of complete terror, shock and panic. Our life, and our children's lives were at stake. We were afraid to speak. We did not know why? For what reason? And we did not know what was going to happen to us, and our two young children. Our children realized the seriousness of the situation. They could hear and see the terrible effect on their loving father. But, they were young and could not fathom the seriousness, or the consequences of this event. They saw us crying a lot, but they were too young to understand why.

This was a horrible, terribly frightening blow to Bern. It would have been a terrible fearful blow to anyone. It was especially frightening for Bern because he loved his job, loved his work. He was a loyal committed employee. He was loved by everyone who worked with him, and for him. He was loved and respected by everyone, especially by the highest military brass at Ft. Monmouth, where he was well known. He was responsible for having hired almost all the civilian engineers at Ft. Monmouth.

For months we huddled quietly together, afraid to talk to anyone, at home or at work. We were especially afraid to talk to relatives, or neighbors on the phone. Afraid because we knew the phones of everyone working at the Fort were being tapped. And, as we later found out, the FBI had been circulating around every neighborhood, and in the entire region, talking to neighbors, friends. Asking questions. Building up files, dossiers. We were completely terrorized, completely fearful. Bern was especially fearful. He knew that he could not find a job in private industry because private corporations during the Cold War working on government contracts required all their employees to have government security clearance. He knew that he must find a business (that did not require security clearance) to be able to support his family. That he could not depend on the government for security to make a living to take care of us.

In the Spring of 1945, after President Franklin Roosevelt's sudden death, Harry Truman became the accidental President. A narrow-minded man, a product of the Prendergast political machine in Kansas City, known historically as a right wing group. His first act in office was to remove from the Roosevelt Cabinet all the appointees who had agreed with Roosevelt's stated "visions" for the future. Truman purged Washington of New Deal visionaries, in order to gain the right-wing Republican support he would need to get elected. One of his first moves was to reauthorize the Internal Review Boards, a government oversight agency, to search out the backgrounds of all government employees. This legislation was sponsored by J.Edgar Hoover, head of the Justice Department at the time, and was passed with full bipartisan support. It was intended to suppress the dissent of citizens who did not agree with the cold war. It was one of the initial actions of the Cold War taken by the new administration. Thus, the new president Truman began a reversal of all of Roosevelt's foreign and domestic policy plans and agenda. He set out an agenda for a complete turnaround, especially of foreign affairs.

This was a difficult, ugly historical period, one difficult to remember because of the long duration and intensity of the Cold War and the twists and turns made by the successive administrations including and up to the present. The Cold War was an aberration. The cold war foreign policy was based on a permanent war economy, a national security state, and the cowboy tactics of McCarthyism, including the witch hunts, and the destruction of lives and careers, and families. It was cowboy triumphalism. The witch hunts we now call McCarthyism were part of the Truman Administration foreign policy. McCarthyism is now a part of the Cold War legacy.

McCarthyism incorporated a climate of fear, of anti-communism, of red-baiting against individuals, when imprisonment was the price one could pay for exercising one's First Amendment right of free speech. A time when families' psyches were being battered by the pressures of fear, insecurity, uncertainty. It was particularly true of those working for the government, since if they lost their security clearance they could no longer get a job-anywhere. They became unemployable. Since most companies were working on defense contracts for the government, their employees needed security clearance. McCarthyism was like an external force that entered the body politic.

Historically, the phenomenon of terrorism and fear, and persecution is an ancient story. It has been practiced repeatedly by sovereign governments for many centuries. In the early 9th century Ethiopian armies castrated their prisoners of war. The Spartan murder of their Plataen prisoners was described by Thucydides 2,400 years ago in great detail. Pizarro's Conquistadors were known to chop the arms off of the Inca soldiers whom they were fighting. In Caesar's Gallic wars, persecution and murder were routine. In our own Civil War, war against the civilian population was a routine matter of policy. Many historians, however, agree that violence against the civilian population in the course of conflict has perverse consequences. Creating a climate of fear has consequences.

The essence of terrorism is to kill or injure opponents in ways specifically designed to cause fear. It is the way to disorganize the society far out of proportion to the number of victims being harmed. The psychological effect is far greater than the number injured. Terrorism creates a climate of panic and fear, which are psychologically effective, as a means to control the population. Its victims easily become demoralized. Current events taking place become incomprehensible, threatening, even nightmarish. The biggest risk we face is our own panic. "Terrorism is intentional violence or the threat of violence perpetrated on a civilian population to inflict fear in the pursuit of a political agenda." (Eric Foner, Professor of History, Columbia University, 2001)

In 1946, Winston Churchill delivered his Iron Curtain speech in Fulton, Mo., in which he said, "communism constituted a growing peril to civilization." This was also part of the buildup of the Cold War as England was a partner with us in

World War II. England also was developing the same foreign policy agenda as the U.S. They too wanted to create consensus in the population in order to use money for reconstruction to build up the military strength. Building up military power as a nation was the number one priority of the Cold War.

Since the 9/11 attacks the U.S is involved in a new war against terrorism. The rhetoric emanating from the administration is attempting to put the country on a war footing. In fact, the country is at war, this time against Iraq. As usual the administration has initiated a propaganda war to create fear—against terrorism, to continue war. We are once more in a climate of fear and terror, in order to repress dissent against the war (against Iraq) and the foreign policy of perpetual wars. The language of finding scapegoats to punish is once more in the news. This is dangerous. The identical language of McCarthyism is being retrieved to propagandize the war on terrorism.

In March 1947, the Truman Doctrine, which was essentially designed to provide economic and military aid to countries supposedly fighting terrorists, was activated in favor of the ruling Junta of Greece. The Greek junta had asked the U.S. for help to suppress a so-called communist uprising. But the real reason was primarily to maintain the Junta in power. Truman was running for election, the first time, since he had been elevated to the presidency, after the sudden death of Roosevelt. He was being advised by Senator Arthur Vandenberg at the time, "to scare the hell out of the American people, if you want to get elected." Ten days later the Congress, now swelled with Republicans, passed the Truman Federal Loyalty Oath. This had the effect of instituting sweeping investigations of all federal employees, probing into their beliefs, interests, family affairs and associations. The Loyalty Oath is a most disputed law.

It was the time of the House Un-American Activities Committee (HUAC) and the prosecution of the Hollywood Ten, and the Hollywood Screen Writers Guild. These were deliberate attacks on prominent people, mostly in the entertainment business, using red-baiting and dragnet investigations. These tactics of repression and subversion have continued on for the next fifty years.

In July 1948, the Truman Administration initiated The Smith Act. J. Edgar Hoover then instituted prosecutions against twelve Communist Party leaders. Even though the CP itself was not illegal. The political strategy was to further induce fear and terror in the American public, in order to pursue the anti-communist crusade.

In 1950 The Truman Administration with the help of the most vicious conservative member of Congress, Senator Pat McCurran, passed the McCurran Internal Security Act. This gave the President complete power to order "dangerous Americans" to be rounded up and imprisoned during an internal security emergency. These were the most "arbitrary dictatorial powers" ever enacted. It was a time when Presidential power could become the law. It provided a dangerous precedent for our country. And, a pattern and precedent for the administration we have today. The fact is, that in spite of these intensive witch hunts, and the savage red-baiting and reign of terror they created, there was never one spy uncovered. There must be a lesson here.

In 1952, Adlai Stevenson, at the start of his presidential campaign referred to Joe McCarthy's scurrilous red-baiting methods as "hysterical putrid forms of slander." The term McCarthyism became a symbol of the entire historical period of the Cold War as it incorporated the virulent witch hunts and red-baiting methods, as well as the expulsion of government employees from their jobs. All that was needed was to charge someone with "disloyalty". The term McCarthyism also now refers to the government's method of using psychological terror and fear to "Scare the hell out of the American people" (Senator Vandenburg). Such methods are now ingrown, inherent in our political system. They are known as "spin". Those who carry on this form of deception or scare tactics are known as "spin doctors".

Although historical periods may not always repeat themselves exactly, there are often many recurring themes. Certain images remain intrinsic to certain events particularly if they leave a residue of damage, or destruction, in the personal lives of the people who have been singled out as victims. The emblems or symptoms of fear and insecurity, (and paranoia) that were evoked during the fifties are appropriate for the present. The idea that even liberals could damage our country from within took hold and became a national psychosis. McCarthyism was a terrible period in our history, McCarthyism inflicted intense, lasting damage on many innocent Americans and to our country. It will always be remembered as the terrible, ugly period of history. As Joseph Conrad said, the heights of civilization could instantly fall into the most barbarous practices against its own citizens.

After the War, Bern had come home from his service in the Navy and returned to his original job as engineer in photographic research, Assistant Director for Photographic Research Labs, at the Signal Corps, at Ft. Monmouth. We were living in The Vail Homes, a government built housing project of individual apartments which housed over 400 families of civilian engineers, and service personnel. Our two children were born there. The project was built like barracks in units of 6 attached apartments with three units around an open court. The court was landscaped and always maintained in good condition. The Vail Homes was a diverse, multi-cultural, friendly. close knit community of highly educated men and women and their young families. All were professionals, scientists and engineers. Many of the women had been teachers, social workers, journalists. All happy working for the government, and for the American Dream of owning their own home in a town with good schools for their children. Although from very diverse social, ethnic, cultural backgrounds it was a harmonious community of people secure in their families, their jobs and their economic future. It was an ideal community in which to live and raise children. A most happy place.

Bern and I, and our two children were a happy thriving young family. He was working as an engineer in photographic research, in work that he loved, for the government. It was civil service job that he knew provided security for his family, After working as a teacher of deaf children I was at home with our two beautiful and bright children, Jane and Jonathan. Our days were spent listening to children's records, singing songs and rhyming, reading stories, playing games, baking cookies. And being outside every day with all the neighbors and their children.

These apartments were heated by coal stoves. The large stoves were in a corner of the kitchen. The coal bin was on the outside wall of the kitchen, it was reached through a swinging door at the bottom of the wall. One of my tasks was feeding the huge coal stove, it meant shoveling the coal from the bin, across the kitchen into the mouth of the stove several times a day. This was our heating system. We kept the stove going 24 hours a day. It was a very efficient system. Our apartment was always warm for the children. Living in The Vail Homes was a happy memorable time for all the families, especially for all the children. Our children have wonderful memories of The Vail Homes.

Then came the worst of times. It was the beginning of the cold war under the Truman Administration and the rise of McCarthyism. With McCarthyism came the destructive and insane years. Bern became a victim of McCarthyism. The result; for our loving closely knit family, for Bern and myself, and our two beautiful and bright children came years of sorrow, disoriented love and disturbed relationships. Relationships on the rocks battered by the sea of fear initiated by McCarthy and his witch hunts. For us it was tragically a time of the heart of darkness. It was a time of a bleak landscape, the world gone mad in the climate of McCarthyism. All our plans and dreams were destroyed.

In this climate of fear, as a closely knit family we were completely terrorized. We suffered shock and innertness, cut off from the rest of the community by silence for months. Although each one went about their daily routine, Bern went to Ft. Monmouth, the children went to school, and I went about my daily chores, we were acting like robots. Each one was trying to cope with this terrible threat to our family. Each one was trying to cope with the shock and the fear. The post traumatic long term effects of this blow of psychological terror on us, on our family relationships, and the fact that our relationships eventually became disrupted, disturbed and dysfunctional did not surface until several years later. It was the tipping point.

We were victims caught in the horrible center, the crucible of McCarthyism. Bern and I, and our two beautiful and bright children were a happy thriving, loving young family before the event. Bern was happy working as an engineer in research, work that he loved, He was loved and highly respected by all the staff, and by the military personnel with whom he worked closely. We had two beautiful and bright children. Then suddenly the sky darkened, as if a moving tornado was descending, the heart of darkness closed in. Our wonderful life was turned into a twisted pile of nerves.

Michael Rogin, historian, author, captured the essence of the McCarthy era, "Some kind of alien external force had entered the body politic, and threatened to destroy it from within." Think of how innocent people are destroyed in time of war. They call it "collateral damage."

The purpose of the government repression and the McCarthy witch hunts, and the fierce red-baiting of the HUAC committee against the Hollywood Ten screen writers, was to create a scare climate, a climate of fear in the country. It was to scare the American people. The real reason was to justify the military build up for the Cold War against the Soviet Union. Both the Truman Administration and Senator McCarthy, as well as J.Edgar Hoover, were united in this bipartisan effort. It was understood within the government.

Arthur Miller said, "An era may be said to be over when its basic illusions are exhausted."

Victor Navasky (The Nation) said, "Although most illusions about communism may be exhausted, the paranoia left over from those years still persists." And Miller, "It's a long, long time ago, only now, after nearly 60 years does some of the feel of that time begin to return. The color and tone of that era are hard to convey. Dickens' London comes more vividly to mind. There was a madness afloat. Not everyone was opposed to fascism." As in previous times of many wars barbarous practices against the country's own citizens had returned.

Many have assumed that McCarthyism died with the death of Joe McCarthy, in 1957, due to alcoholism. In his last year he was finally sanctioned by the U.S. Senate. Nevertheless, the McCarthy tide, i.e., the scapegoating of American citizens continued to swell. Throughout the decades of the Cold War many federal employees were purged from their jobs on fragile evidence, or no evidence; they were simply designated as disloyal. (remember the Truman Loyalty Oath) This pattern was repeated broadly among many other professions. In every profession from teachers to salesmen to linotypists to union leaders to librarians, individuals were fired by their employers in the name of patriotism and loyalty. In spite of this enormous effort, the arbitrary loyalty program never revealed or uncovered spies. But, the smear tactics continued to spread, inflicting severe damage to many innocent American families. We now consider these men and women as the "lost generation."

We were among the first victims of the McCarthy witch hunts, along with other families of engineers and scientists working at government installations who were caught in this national nightmare. This climate of fear and terror had descended on our community of happy, productive, innocent government employees. Joe McCarthy had come to Ft. Monmouth to institute to create a reign of terror and fear. Our lives were endangered, traumatized by the fear and panic. "Hell was spreading all over our nation, like a drop of ink on blotting paper." (Ceszlaw Milosz) The post traumatic effect happened several years later.

This memoir is a compelling story of our family caught in the center of McCarthyism and the McCarthy witch hunts of the 50's, attacked by the intense psychological fear created by the invidious McCarthy and his ruthless practices. For Bern it was the fear of job loss and insecurity and the fear of not being able to protect his family. The memoir draws on the connections between the treacherous political landscape of the 50's, the history of events, persons, place, and time, and the post traumatic long term effect on our family, especially the damage caused by psychological fear in terms of shattered relationships, disoriented love and alienation with our children. And, into the third generation, with our granddaughter. It was indeed extreme with barbarous practices.

Joseph Conrad, famous author, 19th century, understood succinctly that the distinctions between civilized London and "the heart of darkness' quickly collapsed in extreme situations, and that the heights of European civilization could instantaneously fall into the most barbarous practices against its own citizens.

Several years later, when Jane was about 12–13 years old, the effect of the psychological fear and terror we experienced began to surface. This began particularly in her relationship with me. She began to withdraw emotionally, kept to herself, and she seemed to avoid all physical contact. She kept secrets with her father, Bern. It seemed that her insecurity as a little girl had been intensified, increased with the fear and terror we suffered, through the McCarthy witch hunt. It was apparent that Jane's fear and insecurity had metamorphosed into hostility and hatred (toward me). I then became her enemy for life for the next four decades. Even until today. Just as she has had a lifetime of difficulty in being a loving daughter, she has had difficulty being a mother or showing love as a mother. She has difficulty in showing affection, and/or compassion. She avoids display of affection, either toward me, or toward her daughter (our granddaughter).

As for Jonathan, he began to show evidence of problems in his relationships with us, and with women when he was an adolescent, about 17 years. In his relationship with us he began to have temper tantrums, to show infantile behavior. He went through two marriages that ended in failure because of his infantile behavior, unmanageable temper, rage, and anger. He went through many years of making poor decisions, both in his relationships and as well in his career achievements. Even today, his temper tantrums have continued. He does not seem to have any control over the instant temper reaction.

In 1985, Jane wrote a hate letter to "Dear Dad" enumerating a list of complaints against us: I was not a good mother, we did not pay her bill for tuition to Law School, we did not go to her wedding—to her second husband which took place in Scotland, and ending with this analogy, "Clara and Bernie treat their children like dogs, and their dogs like children." It is difficult to conceive of a child's alienation and disoriented love better expressed. The effect on Bern was devastating. From then on until his untimely death he was in deep despair. Both our loving children are intellectually gifted, linguistically talented and professionally high achieving. We have lived in sorrow too long.

From a loving family, parents and two beautiful and bright children, we lived through the crucible of McCarthyism, victimized by the extreme psychological fear and terror, to have our loving relationship with our two children damaged for the rest of our lives. Somehow in this crucible the wires of love and devotion were crossed, love was disoriented, personalities were twisted, and relationships were blown up against the rocks by a rough sea. A family torn apart, now into the third generation, Our granddaughter has suffered from a poor relationship with her mother (daughter Jane) since she was a young child. Three generations of disturbance and disruption of family relationships due to fear and terror in the crucible of McCarthyism.

The historical period of McCarthyism was equivalent to a monstrous nightmare for many American citizens. It remains a marker in our history as a period of devastation, destruction, the savaging of many families by a ruthless demagogue. It is a marker of the political landscape connecting the social and cultural environment with the lives of many people, and the events that shaped their lives. In the 20's individuals who were willing to go to prison for their beliefs were wiped out. They were the "lost generation". In the McCarthy era it was the librarians, teachers, scientists, defense workers, union organizers, all those who lost out in the "red purges" of the 40's and 50's who were the lost generation. It was an era of return to barbarism and ruthlessness against innocent people.

The cultural costs of McCarthyism have never been calculated, and cannot be computed. The costs in damaged and destroyed lives for those caught in the ring of fire of the McCarthy witch hunts and the downloading effects on their lives, and the lives of their children has not been calculated. The fallout has never been fully recorded. And so can never be known.

How many families were affected by the wave of the witch hunts? How many were damaged irrevocably?
How many children were emotionally harmed, left with charred personalities, twisted relationships? And how many victims have passed on their disordered relationships?

This memoir is a reminder of the life of Bernard Maslow, a remarkable man, an extraordinary human being and our loving family caught in the crucible of the McCarthy witch hunts. A personal/historical tragedy. A metaphor for years of the erupting "red" volcano" of McCarthyism. Our fate was hammered and misshapen by powerful political and historical events. How the national tragedy of McCarthyism became our personal nightmare.

McCarthyism bequeathed America much more than an incomplete record. It changed the lives of thousands of people at the same time that it changed the nation's political culture. The McCarthy era shaped our society the crusade touched many areas of American life. But like many severe storms it left a lot of human lives wrecked.

As the eminent playwright Lillian Hellman, who went before the HUAC committee said, "Life had changed everyone."

The Nobel Prize winning poet Czeslaw Milosz said, "More clever than you, I learned my century/pretending I knew a method for forgetting pain." We have lived with the pain of the McCarthy years the rest of our lives.

4

ISAAC'S DREAM: AN ARRANGED MARRIAGE

Classroom of Pre-school at The Vail Homes, Mihala Atchison, Teacher,
1950–52

Long before we met, in the pre-arranged plan of his wonderful father, Isaac, I knew I loved him. He was in my dreams. He was my Prince, come to take care of me. I needed him. It was in the fall, the end of September, the usual time of the Jewish holidays, in Belmar, N.J. a seaside town along the ocean, where my father owned two summer bungalows. Every year, in the fall, after the summer tenants had gone home and the bungalows were emptied, and cleaned, my family usually invited Bern's parents, Lisa and Isaac, and another couple Max and Becky from New York to spend the Jewish holiday week-end with us at the seashore. These two families, who were very old friends, had been coming to visit with us for the holidays for many years.

Usually they came from New York City by train. This time was different.
Bern drove his parents in his car to Belmar. The story is that Isaac had come to my Aunt Ida's funeral in early July, after she died so unexpectedly of cancer. He had always loved Ida, for years, ever since she had come to this country as a young woman at 18 years old. They had been good friends since then. He appreciated her for her talents, and for her intelligence, and as a wonderful person. When she became sick, with cancer, he was the first to come to our house to help. He knew the entire family for many years and he knew me as a young girl. When he returned home he had an idea; he thought of a plan for Bern to meet me. Bern was Isaac's only son, and Isaac had the notion he wanted to arrange for us to marry. He decided that the time of the Jewish holidays when he and Lisa usually came to visit us would be the perfect time. But he had to convince Bern. Bern usually went with his New York friends to the lake region in upper New York State every weekend in summer. He pleaded with Bern to come to meet me. Bern came because he loved his father so dearly and could not refuse his urgent request. Bern drove them to Belmar.

As he got out of the car I saw a slender good-looking young man, with the same wonderful strong face as Isaac, with a head of dark curly hair. As he came close I saw those deep set sparkling sapphire blue eyes under the bushy brows that looked me over; and seemed to look through me. I remember I was wearing my usual summer clothes a pair of home-made, dark green shorts with a red bandana halter top which showed my suntanned, strong body. I was a very strong swimmer in the ocean. We met, we talked, and we went for a long walk on the boardwalk to get acquainted. We were two people each from a different planet, he grew up in the city, I grew up in the country, and at the beach. It was as if we were from different planets, different landscapes. He was a city boy, I was a country girl, a swimmer.

It was the early fall of 1940. In July of that year Isaac had been to our house in New Jersey to attend the funeral of my Aunt Ida, my mother's younger sister. Ida was the second tragedy for my mother and her siblings, who came here as immigrants. At age 39, with two children, Ida was told she had advanced breast cancer. Freda, the younger was still in high school, Jack was in college, at MIT. Ida was operated on, a mastectomy. Two years later the cancer had metastasized to the brain. She was discharged from the hospital and sent home. Our family cared for her at home; by my mother (her sister) Riva, and Rachel (sister-in-law, my father's sister) with care 24 hours a day, round the clock. She lived for another 11 months.

Our family was devastated by her untimely death, at such a young age. And by the fact that she left two children and a husband who was burdened by enormous financial debt due to the high cost of medical care. In those times there was no medical insurance. Families had to bear the entire cost of medical treatment themselves. With serious illness medical care could become a huge financial burden.

Isaac had known Ida, as a close friend since she arrived in this country as a young woman 18, and went to work in the garment industry as a talented sample maker. In the garment shops she met and worked with another woman who was a close friend of Lisa, Bern's mother. She was a frequent visitor in their house and Isaac and Lisa considered Ida one of their very close friends. They were also close friends with the rest of the family, with my parents as well. Isaac was overcome with grief by Ida's untimely death, and he was sensitive to the family grieving, to all of us. He was like a member of our family. When he returned home after the funeral, he apparently had thought of a plan—he wanted to bring Bern and me together, to have Bern meet me. Thus, when my parents invited Isaac and Lisa to spend the Jewish holiday at the seashore with us, Isaac convinced Bern to come along with them. The excuse he gave Bern was that "all the family are broken hearted by this tragedy, Clara is a pretty young girl who needs someone to take care of her."

Bern was from a different place, a different landscape, an entirely different social and cultural milieu. He grew up in New York he went to school in New York he rode the subway to school and to college. Every summer from the age of 7 he went away to summer camp. He was exposed to a rich cultural and social experience all his life with his parents. He was part of a close knit circle of friends, who lived in Brooklyn and the Bronx with the same intellectual and social background. They had also attended the same public schools, and the same summer camp. And grew up with the same intellectual and political perspective. They were a more sophisticated social group. On the other hand, I was from a very different landscape in terms of city versus country, but I still had a background of intellectual and cultural stimulation. I did not have a social group, I did not have many friends. I was more a home-body. Nevertheless, we were attracted to each other. Bern said many times that he fell in love with me as soon as he saw me. Bern went home to New York. Soon he began to visit me in New Jersey every weekend. After Ida's death we lived in an apartment. Freda had to finish school, Jack was out of school and working, and I was working as social worker for the state in Red Bank.

When Bern agreed to come to visit for the weekend, he did not know what he would find. After all, I grew up in farm country. New Jersey was known as the garden state. And when they arrived in Belmar I was playing ball on the lawn with the younger children. I was wearing the skimpiest clothes, and did not look my best. But after we took a walk on the boardwalk and he had a chance to look at me and we talked of serious matters, we began to hold hands. He held my hand in his for the rest of our lives, in the movies, on walks, in concerts, in bed. No one could love me more, and I fell in love with his wonderful strong face and his brilliant sparkling blue eyes. My Prince had come to take care of me.

Bern was working for the U.S. Civil service Commission when we met. The offices were in the federal building downtown New York on Christopher Street near the Village. On the same street nearby was a famous chocolate shop, The Lilac Chocolate Shop. Every week when he came to visit he would bring a box of butter crunch from the Lilac Shop. And, even throughout our life together he always remembered to bring a box of butter crunch chocolate for my birthday.

We were married in March 1942, in Red Bank, N.J., the town next to Ft. Monmouth where Bern was working as an engineer. Not long after we were married, Bern was called by the draft. In spite of his severe hearing loss in both ears, ever since he was a little boy, he was approved by a medical officer and accepted into the Navy. We were shocked that the service would accept him with his handicapping condition. And we were appalled that a medical examiner would approve him for service. But, they accepted him with his hearing loss. He served for three years as engineer at the Norfolk Navy Depot, in Virginia.

Bern returned from service in the Navy to his position as engineer in photographic research in the photo labs for the Signal Corps, at Ft. Monmouth. We lived in the Vail Homes for the next eight years, our two children were born there. This was a government built housing project, of barrack-like apartments and houses built to house the civilian engineers and their families and other service personnel working at Ft. Monmouth. The Vail homes accommodated approximately 450 families. This was a lively, buzzing young community of highly educated, mostly professional men and women. All were young, many had served in the Army or Navy and returned home to work for the government, and to raise a family. Many of the wives had been in professional work, as teachers, social workers, journalists, or in administrative jobs for the government. All of us were busy raising our children with the help of the Baby Book, by Dr. Benjamin Spock, who was our guru as well as a nationally known pediatrician and authority on child-rearing. It was a lively place to be in this environment of young couples, all working to create the best culture for raising our children. And all were focused on soon owning their own home in a community with good schools, to provide for the best possible education for their children.

In this community of alert, intelligent, educated and ambitious women we organized a group to start a pre-school for our young children. The purpose was to have a good nursery school where our children would have instruction in reading and socialization in the best possible educational program. We organized and operated the pre-school. We hired a superb teacher, a young black woman Mihala Atchison, who had been teaching grades one-eight in a segregated school for black children in the next town.. We were fortunate in our choice. The educational program was excellent, we had a class of twenty-five children with the best-possible teacher, who was later hired by the town where she had taught in the segregated school. She was a first grade teacher in the Tinton Falls School for the next twenty-five years. And the elementary school where she taught is now named for her, The Mihala Atchison Elementary School.
Our children were very fortunate. Every child in that class of pre-school children became a great reader, a good achiever all through their school years.

Living in the Vail Homes with our two small children it was truly the best of times. Life was near utopian. We lived a daily happiness with our two bright and beautiful children. We were secure. Bern was in a secure civil service job as an engineer, in work that he loved. He had figured out long before that, with his hearing loss he must have a job with security to provide for his family, and to send his children to college. He wanted to provide for his family in the same way that his father Isaac did for his family. Isaac was his model, his mentor.

In today's societal norms of "boom", in a culture of "global greed", not many people are concerned with having a job with "security". But in our day having lived through a Great Depression with years of unemployment and job insecurity, and for Bern in particular, the knowledge of his hearing loss, it was essential to have a secure job. He always knew that working for the civil service as an engineer would provide the security he wanted. That he could provide for the education of his children and for a life style like the one he was raised in, in Isaac's home.

> "Expect no further word or sign/from me
> Your own will is whole/upright and free
> And it would be wrong/not to do/as it bids you
> Therefore I crown and miter you over to yourself." (Dante)

ROMANCE WITH THE OCEAN LANDSCAPE, WHERE WE FIRST MET AND FELL IN LOVE

"Every person lives his real, most interesting life under the cover of secrecy." Chekhov once said.

The love I share with the ocean is a secret love. Long ago I developed a romance with the large mysterious body of blue water with its pulsing surging curling white waves. The ocean was my first love, my romance with the ocean landscape began when I was very young and learning to swim. My father was my teacher. I remember feeling the embrace of the cool water over my body with its swaying, rhythmic motion as my body was making its own motions through the current. My arms flapping, my legs swinging I can still feel the excitement of the water churning and rolling over me. The ocean is a part of me, I still feel its embrace when I sleep. The ocean, a live rolling throbbing body of water is the metaphor of my life. It is the place where Bern and I met, with the arrangement of Isaac, and fell in love. The ocean's alternating landscapes, its oscillating rhythms, its varying, shifting, moving from calm and smooth to churning and roaring, different during the days and the nights, and the seasons and the year are reflected in the narrative of our life together.

When I was about two, my father, Yalek, who worked as a decorator of fine china at Lenox China, rented his first bungalow in Belmar, N.J., a small town along the ocean with beautiful white sandy beaches all along the coast. We lived in Trenton, N.J., and this was to be our summer house. The town was almost lying in the ocean for its entire length. Our house was about a half mile from the beach. My mother would push me in a baby carriage every day along the path between the wild blueberry bushes to the beach. There I learned to swim with my father holding me up as I kicked my legs and waved my arms. I felt the embrace of the cool, moving water, tasted its salty taste, and felt the rhythm of the churning waves as we pushed against the current. It was then I fell in love with the ocean, with its calming view, its rolling waves, the fascinating feel of breezes at night, the salt on my cheeks. The ocean was in my blood, in my heart.

The ocean, the sea, with its enigmatic varied sensuous landscape of dark images, crashing waves, the sounds like the symbols of the orchestra, and the fragrance of salt spray across my face is in my bones. It embodies the mysteries of other worlds. The night world is one of impregnable depth, undisclosed life beyond view, with roaring, crashing, thundering waves above. Contrasted with the early morning calm, serenity and tranquility. The calm, serene mirror-like expansive surface, reaching across the horizon to the sun rising, with the soft-licking small white waves on the shore. This indefatigable unremitting at times tumultuous ocean and all its sensual vibrations, especially the rhythms of the waves has been strongly imprinted in my consciousness. It is in my senses. So many images so many sensual feelings. It is where I first met Bern, and fell in love. This vibrant, living, dark mysterious, churning, symbols crashing ocean is a part of my blood stream, as is Bern.

Every night, as my eyes are closing, as I am falling asleep, I put down the book, or journal that I am reading. I rearrange the pillows, and turn off the bedside lamp. I am remembering the ocean once again. And, as I am falling asleep, I recall the clear image of the vast mirror-like sparkling ocean in the early morning, and I can feel its calmness, its serenity and the coolness of the water as we swam. Every morning at 6 a.m. I went down to the beach with my father for our early morning swim. The ocean landscape was peaceful, soothingly calm, tranquil, and like a mirror extending into infinity across the earth where it met the brilliant sun just rising in the eastern sky. The sunrise filled the sky and was reflected in the entire surface of the water, a shimmering reflection over the vast surface reaching across the earth.. The water was calm, cool wonderfully soft on the skin, and the tiny little waves on the shore just licked the feet. Swimming was delightful, easy and embracing. The water barely moved in rhythmic motion, as we swam.

We stayed in the water for about an hour every morning. It was a refreshing, memorable time. This early morning ocean landscape with its calm, quiet soothing quality seemed more like a primitive shore in an early biblical setting centuries ago. It is a recurring dream, a vivid remembrance, my love and romance with this wonderful serene ocean landscape.

My father was a strong swimmer, he always entered the water first. He had learned to swim when he was a young boy in Russia at the shore of the Black Sea which was near their home in Baranovka. He always walked into the cool water up to his waist and then started to swim, I followed but took a little time to get used to the water; then I began to swim far out to be close to him. We swam close together. He wanted to be sure I was safe. The ocean was calm, clear and quiet, smooth as glass, only small waves at the very edge that rolled up on the sand and then swooshed back. The vast ocean shimmering with the reflection of the early morning sunrise stretched as far as the eye could see without a ripple. Swimming in the soft cool water was refreshing and calming and soothing for the senses. These early morning swims with my father were unforgettable. A quiet, serene tender memory that has been imprinted for all these years, that served as a firm bonding with my father, and to give me the thoughtful confidence for the troubled times in life. It was my bonding and romance with the ocean early in my life.

The ocean, with its ever transforming landscape, changing its looks, its rhythms, its differing sounds, different salty sprays and smells, its different coolness to the skin, and ordered to the shifting weather at different seasons of the year has formed the latticework of my memories. And, as the images of the ocean landscape varied, differing look, sounds, smells, and touch, at different time of day, time of year, and varying changing weather, these emotions and sensations grew like vines on the latticework.

It was here at the ocean, at end of summer, the time of the Jewish holidays, of Rosh Hashona, and Yom Kippur at my father's bungalow in Belmar (N.J.), and after the summer vacationers had departed, vacated the bungalows, when the landscape was always quiet and peaceful, with soft summer breezes still blowing, and the nights filled with stars that we met, Bern and I. It was a time of crystal clear weather with a serene ocean landscape that you came, with your wonderful father Isaac and mother Lisa to visit us. It was here at the ocean that we first met and fell in love. Where the first evening we went for a walk on the boardwalk and you held my hand in yours, tightly for the first time. And ever after for the rest of our life together. Years later you wrote to our granddaughter, Emily, that you fell passionately in love with me from the moment you saw me. I was wearing dark green shorts, with a red bandanna kerchief as halter, that I had made, revealing my tanned skin. You saw the blonde hair, and fell in love.

I remember the ocean, the sound of the churning waves and the salt spray filled the air that night as we walked on the boardwalk in Belmar, and we talked as you held my hand tightly.

Belmar, is a small community on the New Jersey shore about one hundred miles south of NYC. It is bounded by the ocean from one end to the other, with beaches along the entire length. The winter population is small, mostly the business community, while in summer the population swells with the influx of families from the northern N.J. cities. The families want to enjoy the beaches and ocean swimming with their children. It was here that my father came in the early years to buy property, to build a house. He planned for two apartments so that he could have one for his family for summer vacations, and have an income from the second. He loved the ocean swimming, and he wanted his family, his children, and his grandchildren to love the ocean and to have a place to swim in the summer.

My father, Yalek, as he was called in Yiddish, was born with exceptional artistic and visual talent and skills. When he was a little boy, he would make exact and beautiful architectural drawings. He had excellent eye-hand coordination and drawing skill. He was the oldest of six children born to my grandparents, Aaron and Fradle, or Baba Fradle. (Freda in English) in Baranovka, Russia, a town about fifty miles west of the famous city Kiev. When he was 14, his parents sent him to a fabricant—a factory that made fine china, in Kiev, to learn the art and skills of decorating china When he came to the U.S as a young man, shortly after he and my mother were married, he immediately sought out the finest china company—Lenox China Co. in Trenton, N.J., where he got a job as china decorator. Soon he began to save money from his wages to send for my mother Riva and her mother and siblings for passage to the United States.

My father was a handsome man, intelligent and well educated and ambitious for his family. He knew a great deal about property and building. He knew how to design and construct houses. He had learned from his father, Aaron, who had been in the real estate business in Baranovka. The family lived on a large farm, a beautiful property, with one or more orchards with a large vegetable garden, and with live stock—cows and chickens and ducks, which Baba Fradle managed like an overseer. All six children were well educated, all with different ambitions. The youngest daughter, Tsipa, left home to join the Communist Party. She married a young man who was a lawyer who later became a municipal court judge. They had two sons. All three men were killed in World War II.

My father's first goal was to send passage money for my mother and her mother, The Baba, and the other five siblings to come to this country. They all established residence in Trenton. Then he sent money for passage to his father Aaron and his two brothers and sister, Harry, Shmelyosa, and Rachel. The Baba Fradle died and the youngest brother, Youseff, had migrated to Jerusalem where he died very young, a suicide. Both Shmelyosa and Rachel first migrated to Jerusalem to fulfill their ambition to live and work on a Kibbutz in the new Jewish homeland. They remained there a few years and then came to live in the U.S.

After providing passage for my mother, her mother, The Baba, and the five siblings, and his father, Aaron, and siblings, my father sent money for passage to his cousin Anne Meyerson, and her two brothers. When all his family and loved ones were here he then was able to think about his life long wish to buy a piece of land near the ocean, and to build a house for his family to be near the sea in summer. Ever since he was a young man and discovered the joy and pleasure of swimming in the Black Sea, in Russia, he dreamed of having a house near the ocean where he could bring his family for summer vacations. He loved the ocean, he loved looking at the ocean, and swimming in the ocean. His greatest ambition was to have a house near, or at the edge of the ocean for his children and grandchildren. He took great pleasure as each of his grandchildren learned to swim.

The first year, when I was only eighteen months old, my father found his way to Belmar, N.J. He and my mother rented a bungalow. The house was at least a half mile from the beach. In those days, the houses in all the communities along the New Jersey coast were built a distance from the beach. The space between the houses and beach was covered with wild blueberry bushes. Every day my mother would push me in the walker over the path that wound through the bushes to the beach. And, my father would walk down the path to the beach to go swimming. My mother and I sat on a blanket on the sand to watch him. When I was two years old my father took me in the water and held me as I learned to swim.

The towns all along the New Jersey shore north to south were sparsely populated at that time. The coastline communities were mostly for fishing and later were developed for tourism. There was no main road or highway along the coast. That was just being developed and built. It was completed a few years later. The wide strip of bushes separating the houses from the beaches soon became built up with houses to meet the needs of tourism. The streets and houses were extended to the beaches in every community along the coast to meet the swell of tourism that was already taking place. Most of the summer people were families from the northern N.J. cities. They came in droves with their children to spend the summer vacation as soon as school was over. They rented the bungalows for the summer from July 4th until Labor Day.

As a boy growing up in Russia my father learned when he was young about owning property, the personal economic benefit, and also the fact that property could be a source of income. He learned all this from his father Aaron who had what could be called a real estate business. They owned a large farm property, his mother managed the farm and home, and children, while Aaron took care of the business. My father knew that property near the ocean was desirable and valuable, and that if he built a structure of two apartments the income from the second apartment would leave us an apartment without cost. Our family would have an apartment practically rent free every summer. He set about drawing up the architectural plans for this building.

The first property my father bought in Belmar was on 13th avenue. The lot was the second lot from the corner of Ocean Avenue, and across from the beach. It was about 40 feet wide and 200 deep. My father figured that he could divide the lot in half and put a two apartment building on each part. That is how he designed the building, one apartment on the first floor, another on the second floor. The first floor was always rented, and we lived on the second floor. The second floor had a covered porch that extended the width of the building. Standing on the porch, one could actually see the ocean. And at night you could see the stars sparkling across the sky and hear the waves crackle and roar as they broke along the shore. You could feel the salt breeze carried on the wind. And, you could feel the live presence of the ocean with its sounds and smell as it changed through the night. These are haunting, vivid, unforgettable memories.

Every summer at the close of school my father brought our family my mother, brother and me, to Belmar to stay in the apartment for the entire summer. My aunt Ida's two children, Jack and Freda, also came to stay for the summer. My mother and Ida were two very devoted sisters, two hearts as one. Ida was married to my father's brother Harry: two sisters married two brothers. The four children grew up together as one family. I had two mothers, two wonderful women as mothers. We were all bonded closely as sisters and brothers. Our relationship was patterned on the strong bonding and devotion that was in our mother's family, between the grandparents and their children.

Every Friday evening my father came from work with his car filled with goodies. He would stop at the bakery on the outskirts of Trenton to buy a very special cinnamon bread, and then at a farmer's stand to buy flowers, the tall brilliant Russian sage flowers. As well as the farm grown vegetables. These were the exceptional New Jersey corn, tomatoes, eggplants, beans, and melons. He was a proud man who was happy to provide for his family. He enjoyed being with us at the ocean, and providing the wonderful food every week. My children still remember the delicious cinnamon breads from the bakery in Robbinsville. They have fond memories of their days at the beach and learning to swim in the ocean.

Every Saturday night Ida and Harry came for the weekend, after they closed their store in New Brunswick. They came with the car loaded with all kinds of good food, as well. Ida was a superb baker and cook. She usually baked Danish yeast cake with apricot filling, several large loaves to feed the family. They also brought home made cheeses, and milk and eggs from the farms near them. And they always stopped at the wayside farm stands to bring fresh corn and tomatoes and vegetables.

During the 30's, 40's, New Jersey was known as the Garden State. Practically the entire state, except for the populated cities in the northern region, was planted with large orchards; large berry farms in the southern region, and the entire middle of the state was planted with fields of corn and tomatoes as far as the eye could see. The Jersey soil was especially fertile in texture and nutrients such as nitrates necessary for the sweetness of the corn and the tomatoes. No other state could compare in flavor of its corn and tomatoes. Our parents, who grew up in the eastern Crimea region of Russia an agricultural region where the soil is very fertile, where vegetables and fruits are grown were delighted to find the excellent produce grown in New Jersey where they had settled. They used to talk frequently about the wonderful fruits and vegetables they had as children, growing up with orchards in their own yard. They were delighted to find the excellent quality and taste of the Jersey produce. They were also knowledgeable about nutrition, and wanted to provide their families with the most nutritious foods.

Every night during the summer the four of us, my brother and I and Freda and Big Jack (Ida's children) slept on the long open porch (on the second floor). My mother and I would open the four army cots, cover them with warm blankets and we would sleep under the endless black sky and stars. We could hear the ocean waves break against the shore and feel the salt spray on our faces. Falling asleep to the rhythm of the ocean waves is an unforgettable memory. Even now when I am falling asleep I can still feel the rhythms of the breaking waves and hear and smell the ocean. These magical sensations are imprinted on my memory. The feelings of sleeping on a cot wrapped warmly under the sky listening to the breaking ocean waves and feeling the cool salt air on my face is embedded in me.

My mother Riva, as she was known in Baranovka, or Eva, the Americanized name, was the oldest of six children of Jacob and Bella, my grandparents. Ida was the next oldest, two years younger than my mother, and then came the three boys and Sara the youngest. Jacob and Bella were known as exceptionally loving people, unusually good, kind and generous of spirit. They were like two loving doves. Jacob was a pillar of the synagogue, known as an intellect, a reader of the Torah, who spent a good deal of time discussing the meaning of the Torah and other philosophical issues. At home he had a shop attached to the house, where he designed and made shoes. He was a talented creative designer.

Jacob and Bella were extraordinarily warm and generous and well known in the region. Bella, The Baba, as we called her, was known to share the family's food with anyone in need. The parents were exceptionally devoted and the children were also devoted, like peas in a pod. They were totally committed to each other. They were all intelligent and educated. All were warm loving and generous people

My mother Riva was known in the region as a beautiful woman, with thick red hair, blue eyes, a peaches and cream complexion and a beautiful figure. She married my father, Yalek, a handsome man, the oldest of six children in his family. My father left for the U.S. soon after they were married. Ida was known for her extraordinary talents as a dress designer and dressmaker, which she inherited from her father Jacob. In appearance she resembled her mother, The Baba, a petite woman with lovely brown eyes and brown hair. All the siblings in my mother's family were quiet, soft spoken, gentle personalities. All were extremely generous.

Jacob died of the flu in the epidemic of 1905. Soon after my father sent money for passage to the U.S for my mother, The Baba, and all five siblings. He had saved the money for their passage from his wages as a china decorator at the Lenox China Co. The family came to Trenton, N.J., to settle there. Ida soon found her way to NYC where, with her expertise as a dressmaker/designer she landed a job in the garment industry as a sample maker.

The garment industry in New York City was just beginning to grow into the immense monolith it would become for the next fifty years. The dress shops were filled with women, all experienced dressmakers, mostly immigrants, mostly from the Ukraine region of Eastern Europe. Soon after beginning work in the dress shop, Ida made friends with two women working in the same shop. They lived in Brooklyn. They became life long friends. Two in particular became important in Ida's life, and in mine as well. One was Minnie, and the other was Lisa. Lisa was married to Isaac, they were the parents of Bern and his sister. Minnie's sister Becky, and husband Max also became life long friends. Ida introduced these friends to my parents, who then became their life long friends as well.

My mother and Ida continued their close friendship with these two couples over the years. During the winters they visited in NYC, they met at concerts and other cultural events. In summer their children went to camps in the mountain and lake regions of New York State. They grew up with camp songs, sharing bunks with life long friends, canoeing, playing tennis, listening to concerts. While my family spent summers at Belmar, swimming in the ocean.

For the four of us, my brother Little Jack and I, and Freda and Big Jack, growing up spending summers at the ocean gave us wonderful memories. My son, Jonathan, now a grown man, a professional editor, still loves the ocean. "Mom, I am still an ocean kid." He lives in New Jersey, in Cape May County, the southern most county, about 10 miles from the beach. He loves to go swimming daily.

Every summer after Labor Day, after the tenants in my father's bungalows would leave, my father would have the bungalows cleaned spotlessly. My parents and Ida invited their friends Max and Becky and Lisa and Isaac to spend the Jewish Holidays with us in Belmar. These dear friends came every year. All the summer people had left. The ocean landscape was now calm and peaceful, back to its primitive beauty. It was quiet, the weather was always good. It was like living in a dream world.

In July 1940, my aunt Ida died of brain cancer. It had started three years before with breast cancer. She had a radical mastectomy. Three years later the cancer had metastasized to the brain. This tragic event was the most painful blow to our family, a group of loving, devoted caring people, and especially to my mother, the oldest who considered herself responsible for her sisters and brothers. She had promised her father Jacob, as he was dying of the flu that she would take care of the family. This was a horrible tragedy for a family of young immigrants.

In the 30's, 40's and even into the 50's little was known about cancer, except that it was a painfully slow and terrifyingly painful death. Most people did not know about the need for early detection, or, as in the case of breast cancer the need for self-examination. And, the medical profession itself had not recognized the use of chemotherapy to prolong life, or even to prevent the inevitable death. To my mother and the other siblings, Ida's illness was an unfathomable, unendurable misfortune. We simply could not bear it.

After the second operation Ida survived for nine months. My mother came to live in Ida's house to care for her. My aunt Rachel, my father's sister, gave up her job as nurse in a Brooklyn hospital, to come stay with us and take care of Ida. They took care of her, nursed her round the clock and kept her alive for almost a year. Remembering the love and care and devotion of my mother, and Rachel, and the other members of the family during those last months of caring for Ida remains a painful, overpowering memory.

For my mother and our closely knit and tightly bonded family of immigrants, Ida's death at such a young age ravaged by cancer, was an unbelievably painful tragedy. Her long-suffering death and her loss reverberated in every family member, including the youngest children. We were a grieving family stranded on a rock of unfathomable depth stunned and unbelievably injured. An everlasting pall had fallen over us, and for years to come. The memory does not die.

Ida was the talent, the mentor, the idol of the family. She produced beauty in everything, in designing and making clothes (for all of us), in decorating her house with the most beautiful linens and fabrics from the best most artistic sources in the world, and in gardening and landscaping her yard. In her love of culture, of concerts, museums and great art, she was gifted, talented, a superb mentor and teacher. My mother was head of the family. Together with Ida they served as father, mother and caretaker of the family. This was a remarkably close interwoven relationship. To know them was to admire them, to respect and love them. Knowing them and their devotion one can understand a small part of the incomparable grief and despair when she died, so young. As if some force had torn her away from us.

I was in my early twenties when Ida died. She was my second mother, my mentor, my idol. From the age of five, I started watching carefully at her table where the material was spread out and she would sketch out the parts of the pattern on the fabric. And then cut. She never needed or used a store bought pattern, the pattern was in her head. The shape of the parts, the angles, the dimensions, the size, was sketched in her mind. With scissors she flew over the fabric rapidly. She knew exactly how to sketch and cut. The designer talent at work. Then, amazingly, the parts of the pattern fit perfectly together ready for basting and sewing. I watched this process for days and years, as I slowly learned to baste, to sew together on the machine, and to do the finishing sewing by hand. I learned how to make the most beautiful dresses, and coats and suits. I learned how to use trimmings, exquisitely beautiful insertions and pleating, and edgings to make original creative touches. I learned how to decorate.

I learned from Ida how to design, cut and sew beautiful cloth into designer dresses, to make beautiful tucked and trimmed ladies' blouses, and how to design children's dresses. I learned how to decorate with beautiful cloths, imported linens, velvets and cottons and silks, how to make draperies, bedspreads and tablecloths. And it was Ida who taught me to love literature, music, art sculpture, to enjoy the ballet theatre, and exhibitions. And, it was from Ida I developed my interest and love of gardening, landscaping, architecture, and the love of cooking and baking. Every activity, including my professional work, my interests was all rooted in my love of Ida. All my talents and creative work germinated from Ida.

The longer I practiced, and I have been practicing a lifetime, the more I realized what an exceptionally creative talent Ida had. And I appreciate her infinite creativity and talent in creating beauty in everything she touched. She was my idol, my teacher, she was a part of me, a part of my identity. Ida was in my consciousness always. Just as the wonderful ocean the vibrant mysterious sea is in my consciousness.

Isaac, Bern's wonderful father came to Ida's funeral in New Jersey. He had known Ida since she was a young woman just arrived in America. She worked in the garment industry alongside Lisa, Bern's mother. Isaac was a very good friend, he admired Ida greatly as an exceptional individual, an exceptionally talented woman, a cultured and intellectual woman. Isaac was personally devastated by Ida's death at such a young age. He knew what this loss meant to our family. He was deeply moved and grieving. After the funeral he began thinking that he wanted Bern, his most precious son, to meet me. He had known me when I was a young child but now he saw me as an adult, as an attractive, sympathetic, family member. He wanted Bern to meet me, and to marry me.

At the end of that summer, after Labor Day, after the tenants had left, Isaac and Lisa and Bern came to Belmar to stay for the weekend of the Jewish Holidays. It seems Isaac had persuaded Bern to come to meet me. Bern drove them in his car from Brooklyn. They arrived at mid day. I was playing ball with the younger children. I was wearing green shorts and a halter top that I had made of a red bandana handkerchief. I looked like a farm girl, with my light blonde hair and suntanned body.

Out of the car stepped this slim young man with black curly hair, and as he came up close I saw his beautiful, deep set sparkling sapphire blue eyes. I had never seen such extraordinary, deep blue eyes. Bern looked just like his father Isaac, a handsome face with the same soft voice and gentle manner. We spent the next few days getting acquainted swimming in the ocean during the day and walking on the boardwalk at night He held my hand tightly in his. We sat on a bench watching the magic of the deep dark ocean at night. He told me about his friends, all of whom he had met at the children's camp he attended when he was young. Now these friends were all working in New York. Most were teaching.

They went every weekend in summer to the adult camps in the mountain and lake region of New York state. As we walked he took my hand and held it tightly. He held my hand tightly and took special care of me the rest of our lives.

We met at the ocean, we walked and held hands on the boardwalk facing the ocean, breathing the ocean air, listening to the roll of the waves on the beach, gazing at the ocean at night. Feeling the damp salty spray on our faces; We fell in love. It was at this indefatigable changing ocean landscape, and the rhythmic churning waves that our spirits were united. It was at the ocean that our two beautiful children were born and that we spent every summer as they were growing up. My father took care that we always had a place to stay near the ocean, with our children, his grandchildren.

I have watched this extraordinary magical ocean over many years, a lifetime, as it invariably transforms its ever-changing landscape: different images, different sounds, different moods. I can still see and feel the ocean in the early mornings at 6 am when I went swimming with my father. The immense stretch of sparkling mirror-like water, the calmness, the quiet, the early morning rising sun, the brilliant glow in the sky and the dancing reflection on the surface of the water. And I can feel the coolness of the water against my skin as we swam. My father and I every morning at 6.

I can still see the ocean at night with its dark mysterious impenetrable image and the great rolling thundering crashing white waves breaking far out. I can feel and hear the ocean as we slept on the open porch in Belmar as children. I still feel the cool salty spray on my cheeks as we lay between blankets on cots on the open porch. I can hear the ocean waves breaking against the shore and swooshing as they returned. The immense space, the vastness, the dark, mysterious depth, the churning, the roaring, the whispering, the calmness. These are recurring images still in my mind.

Bern was a part of me, part of my consciousness, a part of my bloodstream for all these years. My life was filled with him, I felt complete, Just as the ocean is still a part of me. I am with Bern my love in the cradle of the rolling waves, like the gentle receding waves on the ocean of the heart.

5

THE EARLY YEARS, A HAPPY LIFE

From the time our children, Janie and Jonathan were born, my father Yalek (Louis), made certain that we had an apartment for the entire summer at the beach, in Belmar, N.J. Belmar is a small town on the New Jersey coast about ten miles south of Asbury Park. Its entire eastern side is coastline with wide, open beaches. Our apartment was on the second floor with a long open porch. We were only one half block to the beach.

We were there every summer as a family when the children were growing up. Our house was so close to the beach we could see the vast blue ocean, smell the salt spray in the breeze and listen to the throbbing breaking waves along the shore. At night it was magical, sitting on the porch under the sky filled with stars, breathing the salty moist air, listening to the crashing of the waves, the roaring sounds. It was as though we were embraced by nature, nestled into the waves. Bern commuted daily to his work at the Ft. Monmouth Photo Research Labs. This was about three-quarter of an hour ride. Life was beautiful, life was peaceful.

Waking up every morning to see the bright sun coming up in the east over the ocean, the smell of the sea, the striking rainbow, the morning smell of coffee. Our children, Janie and Jon bright and happy going out to play every morning. We went to the beach every afternoon. The children played near the water's edge building sand castles with the edge of the waves washing their feet. I took each one in my arms into the waves. In this way each one learned to stand up in the waves and to paddle and to swim. It was the greatest fun for them. It was how my father had taught me to swim.

Both children became good swimmers. Jonathan is an exceptional swimmer like I am, and like Yalek, my father. Jon loves the ocean like I do. When he decided to live in New Jersey he bought a house in Dennisville, Cape May County. His house is 10 miles from the ocean beach where he swims daily. As he said recently, "Mom, I'm an ocean kid. I love the ocean, I was raised at the ocean and that is where I love to live."

During these early years, as the children were growing up, my father Yalek was still working as a China Decorator at the (famous) Lenox China Ltd. He lived in Trenton, N.J. the home of Lenox. Every Friday afternoon, after he finished work, he bathed and dressed carefully, prepared for the long drive to Belmar. On the outskirts of Trenton, in the small town of Robbinsville he stopped in the bakery to buy a wonderful cinnamon bread which he brought us every week. Then further down the road at a farm stand he bought fresh corn, beefsteak tomatoes, and peppers and eggplants. Deep shiny purple things. And, always, a big bunch of flowers, usually Russian Sage, with huge deep crimson leaves. These were famous products of N.J., the garden state.

My father Yalek loved his children and his grandchildren. He was so proud of us. He came every Friday evening to be with us and to work on his bungalows. He ate every meal with us. He was a quiet man, not talkative, with a good sense of humor, and very intelligent. He did not express his love easily but he showed us every Friday with his big smile and arms full of gifts.

On Saturday and Sunday, I usually made special breakfast for my father and family. And for dinner we had fresh fish from the ocean. Usually it was blue fish. At that time of year the schools of blue fish were "running" close to the shore. They were practically on the beach. Often our neighbor Dave gave us the fish he caught. He would go surf fishing on the beach every weekend. Like a true fisherman he cleaned the fish perfectly. All I had to do was drop them in the frying pan. We always had fresh Jersey corn, and sliced sweet beefsteak tomatoes that my father brought. This was our typical summer menu.

On the week ends my father Yalek worked on the bungalows doing carpentry and construction. Some kind of repair was always needed because of the salty air. Jane and Jon looked forward to grandpa coming every Friday afternoon, with all the goodies. And, especially they remember the cinnamon bread. They still talk about this. Grandpa Yalek was an important part of our family. The children knew him. They knew how much he loved them. Life was good, for all of us.

AND THEN THERE WAS BECKY AND MAX

Becky and Max were old friends of Bern's parents in Brooklyn since before they were married and before they had children. Lisa (Bern's mother) had worked in the garment industry making expensive ladies blouses. There she met Becky's sister, who also worked in the same shop. When my Aunt Ida came to work in the garment shops and met Lisa, Bern's mother, they became good friends. Lisa introduced Ida to Becky's sister and they became good friends. Ida considered both couples her best friends. Soon after, Ida introduced my parents to Lisa and Isaac, and to Becky and Max. Isaac was especially close to Ida. He admired her, respected her, and knew how talented she was.

Our families became good friends forever. Lisa and Isaac had two children, Sophie and Bern, Becky and Max had two children, Leo and Rose. Bern and I were friends with Leo and Rose. We were the younger generation.

Before Bern and I were married Max and Becky moved to New Jersey to the town of Allenhurst, on the Jersey Shore. Max had retired, he had sold his business in Brooklyn, and bought a paper route in Allenhurst. They lived about 25 minutes ride from our house in Belmar in the summer. And about the same distance to our house in winter.

Max used to work on his paper route every morning early, starting at about 5 a.m. By noon his work was complete for the day. After lunch, he and Becky came to visit us to play with the children. Every day Jane and Jon looked forward to being with Becky and Max, they were a part of our family, like another set of grandparents, bonded with them. Becky and Max were a part of our life, included in everything. They had supper with us every night. They went home when the children were ready for bed.

When our children, Jane and Jonathan were growing up they were circled by a chain of family and friends, both from Bern's side and from my side, always present, always showering them with affection, warmth and love. They were bonded with love from everyone. And they saw nothing but love and kindness. Max and Becky were exceptional people of my parents' generation. They were warm, kind loving people who loved us and our children as their own. Our children had the advantage of being raised in this warm milieu of family and friends, who loved them and who thought they were the brightest stars in the universe.

AND THEN THERE WAS RACHEL, AND SHMELYOSA, AND HARRY

From the time of his first paycheck, as China Decorator for Lenox China, all alone in this country, my father began to save money to send to Russia for the passage of my mother Riva, and her family; The Baba, and the five siblings—Ida, Herman, Ben, Sara and Sam. After I was born, he continued saving for the passage of his family: His Father Aaron, and the siblings, Harry, Rachel and Shmelyosa. After them, he brought over his cousins, Anna Meyerson and her two brothers.

Soon after they arrived, Harry (Yalek's brother) was married to Ida (my mother's sister). The two older brothers married the two older sisters. My father's sister Rachel moved to Brooklyn where she went to work as a nurse in a maternity hospital. Shmelyosa, the next brother, went to work on a farm in Freehold. They never married. After ten years Shmelyosa finally went back to Palestine to work on a Kibbutz. He had always wanted to work on a Kibbutz. During the war years, War II, he served in the Israeli Army Intelligence. Rachel worked here as a nurse for twenty five years. She remained close to her brothers Yalek and Harry and she was especially devoted to their children.

Rachel came to visit us, to be with Jane and Jon at least once a month, on her day off. She called often to speak to the children to keep in touch. She wanted to know every time they sneezed. She was so devoted, she cared so much, about her brothers, about us, and about our children. We were her life. And our children Jane and Jon loved her as well. Jane's daughter Emily, our granddaughter is named after Rachel (Emily Rachel). After twenty-five years Rachel retired from the Brooklyn Hospital. She went to join Shmelyosa, to live in Israel to be near him. She continued to work there as a nurse, until retirement. When Emily, our grandchild, Jane's daughter, was four, Bern arranged for us—Jane, Emily and I to go to Israel to visit Rachel. Janie wanted Rachel to see Emily, who shares her middle name. It was a memorable trip for us to be with Rachel whom we all loved.

My brother and I, Yalek's children, and Freda and Big Jack, Harry's children were loved by Aunt Rachel as if we were her very own; she was passionately devoted. And my children, Jane and Jon were loved by Ida and Harry as well. Our children were in a closely-knit family, a warm loving family, bonded to uncles and aunts, and great uncles and great aunt, and by our parents' friends who were like additional grandparents. They were very much loved by their great Aunt Rachel, and great uncles Shmelyosa and Harry.

Both Jane and Jonathan were born while we lived in the government housing project The Vail Homes. This was a very special place with special memories for them.

AND THEN, AFTER THE WAR, THE VAIL HOMES, A WONDROUS COMMUNITY

In Dickens' words, "It was the best of times, it was the worst of times. It was the age of wisdom, it was the age of foolishness". "It was a time when people continued to wonder and imagine." For Bern and me, and our two young beautiful and bright children it was clearly the best of times. It was just after the war the factories were heating up, businesses were booming, everything was blooming, and the landscape was rich with the promise of a good life. Most people had jobs, most were buying cars, and buying houses. Bern had returned from service he was working in his former job that he loved as an engineer for the federal government. And we were living with our two children in a wondrous community, The Vail Homes.

It was after the War. Bern had come home from his service in the U.S. Navy, where he served as a mechanical engineer at the Norfolk Navy Depot. The fact of his having been accepted by the draft board was a shock to us. He had had a hearing loss in both ears since he was a child and he was considered partially deaf. When he was a very young boy he had a history of frequent ear infections in both ears. It was the custom then for doctors to pierce the membrane to allow the fluid to drain. Those were the years before there were antibiotics to treat infections. The result was that both ear drums developed scar tissue which prevented them from vibrating. This caused Bern to have severe hearing loss in both ears: 40% and 50%. We never expected that Bern would pass the physical exam at the U.S. Army Recruitment Center, let alone that he would be inducted for duty. But, he was, and served as a fine engineer in the U.S. Navy.

Bern was intellectually superior, he had IQ in the superior range. He finished high school at age 15, with perfect scores on the NY State Regent Exams in English and Math. He went to City College of N.Y. (CCNY), he finished college at age 19. Then he went on to get a Master's Degree in Mechanical Engineering. At age 20, he went to work as an engineer for a private firm. But because of his hearing problem he was interested in working for the government because it meant security for his family for the future. He passed the Civil Service exam easily and soon he went to work at the U.S. Civil Service Commission in NYC in Personnel, in charge of recruiting civilian engineers for the Signal Corps, at Ft. Monmouth, N.J. After the war he was transferred to Ft. Monmouth to serve as Assistant Director, Photographic Research Laboratory.

We were married shortly before his service on March 12, 1942. We moved to The Vail Homes when I was pregnant with Jane, in 1944.

The Vail Homes was a government built housing project at Ft. Monmouth, N.J. It was located just off the military base in the town of Eatontown, N. J. It was built in 1942 by the U.S. Army Signal Corps to house the civilian engineers needed to work at the Research Laboratories during the time of the war build up. Approximately 400 civilian engineers, physicists and mathematicians and support personnel were hired in a short time. The engineering staff was increased by ten-fold to help fulfill the government contracts of the Signal Corps made in the rush to develop communications instruments needed for the war effort. Bern and I were lucky to get one of the apartments.

The housing development had a very pleasant design, a friendly village layout. The basic design was a courtyard surrounded by three long buildings. Each building was designed with six four-room apartments attached. A four-room bungalow apartment on each end, in the center there were two duplex apartments. Each building had four families, a total of 12 families surrounding each courtyard. This pattern was repeated throughout the housing complex. The entire complex housed about 425 families. It was like a village with streets and houses. The post office was in the town of Eatontown, and the town also provided police protection. The Eatontown police made regular rounds.

Our apartment was an end bungalow four small rooms on one level. It was facing the road. Heating was by a large coal burning stove in the kitchen. Each kitchen had its own stove in one corner on an inside wall. The coal bin, which contained the coal was on the opposite outside wall. The coal had to be shoveled from the coal bin into the coal stove, and the fire had to be maintained around the clock. The coal furnace was like a voracious beast, it had to be fed regularly, round the clock. Consider the fact that every family, every apartment had its own coal stove for heating. Everyone stoked the fire. And everyone in the community was grateful to have such a good place to live with their families since it was wartime.

The rooms were small, the furnishings sparse. Along with a table and four chairs in the kitchen with the coal stove, it was crowded. In the living room we had a second hand lounge chair, picked up at a second hand store, and recovered. We had a day bed given to us by my father, and a long bookcase covering the wall, to house the children's record player and all our books. We had a large collection of children's books and records, which we played every day, and books we read daily.

Among the children's records we had The Nutcracker Suite, and many other songs from children's plays. We had company every weekend. My father stopped in to bring us cinnamon-raisin bread, and other goodies. My mother and Bern's mother came to visit often, and Freda, my cousin-sister came every weekend. The day bed in the living room was in frequent use. The children were extremely happy in this wonderful environment.

The Vail Homes was a very special community, in terms of its friendliness, its unity, and its wonderful spirit of generosity. All the families living there were civilian employees of the government. Everyone was enthusiastic about their work, and they were all loyal citizens. We were all raising our young children and helping each other with everything—with chores, shopping, child-care, nursing care, etc. There was a General Store so that the mothers with young children did not have to travel outside the community. And, there was a pharmacy, and a medical station with a nurse on duty.

A REAL FIND
Almost every family had young children. Most of the women were highly educated, most had worked as professionals before the war; as teachers, social workers, nurses, journalists, etc. Every one was reading the newly published Dr. Spock's Baby Book, and discussing each and every word. Everyone was learning to cook, from the new Settlement Cook Book (Ed. 1942), and swapping recipes.

Every afternoon, after nap time, all the children and mothers congregated around the courtyard. The children played, the mothers talked—exchanging recipes, children's clothes, what does Dr. Spock say? It was the best of times, raising our children, in this warm, friendly sharing community.

Before long many of our children were four years old, ready for some form of pre-school. A group of us educated professionals got together to discuss starting a pre-school. There was Minna Lee, wife of Bernie Lee, my Bern's boss (Director of Photographic Research Laboratory) who had a daughter, Debbie, our Jane's age. There was Ann Bady, former journalist and author, who had a daughter, Susan, Jane's age. There was Elsie Nachmias, a former high school science teacher with a daughter, Barbara, and a few more women with similar credentials and children of pre-school age. We met for several months, we discussed what we thought the curriculum/program should be for a good pre-school. And we discussed what qualifications we should look for in a teacher. We prepared the plans, and presented them to The Vail Homes Housing Committee. The plans were readily approved. After all, we were all professionals involved in this planning. Now we had to find a teacher.

We were extremely lucky, although we were unaware of it. In the very next town of Tinton Falls adjoining Eatontown on one side for many years there was a totally segregated one room school house for the Black children, grades one through eight. The young woman teacher was Mihala Atchison. She taught a handful of children in each grade. On the other side was Red Bank. In the early 1800's, the wealthy people living in New York came across the Hudson River to New Jersey to vacation in this area. They lived in the Atlantic Highlands and in Red Bank, which were the wealthy communities. Their maids and chauffeurs and their families lived in Tinton Falls, a poor town in those days. The town originally had a segregated school for the Black children.

As it happened, luckily for us, the State of New Jersey had recently passed legislation to stop segregation in all schools. Mihala was free. We interviewed her, and hired her immediately. She was an outstanding, exceptional teacher, A master teacher, with all the knowledge and experience of how to teach a pre-school class. She was a great find for us for our pre-school class.

Mihala Atchison was married to a minister of a black church and lived in Newark, N.J., a northern city about three-quarter hour ride. Every morning, at

6:30 a.m. she took the train to Red Bank, and then a cab to our school. She was the right choice, a superb teacher. She taught our children in The Vail Homes pre-school for the next two years. After that, she was hired as First Grade teacher by the Tinton Falls Schools, the same town where the segregated school was, and she taught there for the next thirty years. The primary-elementary school of Tinton Falls School district has been named The Mihala Atchison Elementary School, after their most prominent teacher.

Our Vail Homes Preschool started in September, just as our Janie turned five. There were twenty-five children in the program. It seemed that overnight our children were reading, reading everything in sight. They all loved school. As the families eventually moved out of the housing development into the surrounding suburban towns our children became high-achieving students, top performers. All became professionals. Our children have very wonderful, fond memories, happy memories of living in The Vail Homes attending school. They remember their wonderful teacher Mihala Atchison.

The community of The Vail Homes was a warm, friendly, hospitable place to live for families, children and adults. It was a model in the manner of John Dewey, a remarkable experiment in democracy. It could be called a utopian community. Everyone was in one boat pulling together, loyal, patriotic. Our husbands were working at jobs they loved, for the government. Our families and children thrived in this environment. It was a very special place. There was a congenial atmosphere, we felt a togetherness, as if in a sea of good people all working together. Everyone was kind and generous, and giving. Our children started life in this green garden climate, in a warm supportive environment. This was their social landscape of the early years.

The Vail Homes was a peaceful, integrated community of highly educated professional engineers and their families. All were committed to their work for the government, and were happy in their work. All were working for the American Dream to save money for a home of their own and to send their children to a good school. It was the best of times for all of us. Just as Dickens wrote.

6

THE PRODUCTIVE YEARS: LOVE AND CHILDREN, AN IDYLLIC TIME

Clara and Bernard Maslow, 1984

Bern was an exceptional man, a rare intellectual human being, who was passionately in love with his family. He was of singular devotion in taking care of us, to provide for us in the style and manner that his father Isaac had provided for their family. It was after the horrendous McCarthy witch hunt hearing.. Everyone was glad that McCarthy was dead. Bern had finally resumed his job that he loved with the government at Ft. Monmouth. There was a good feeling in the country. It was over. People happily returned to living a good life—the American Dream. It was a memorable time for us, two people in love, with two beautiful bright children to take care of. Our time for raising a family and a time for productive work.

The horrendous onslaught of the Army-McCarthy witch hunt hearings at Ft. Monmouth had been a significant blow to Bern personally. It affected his entire being. He felt his entire life was attacked, his life of caring for his family. As soon as he was able to absorb the immediate shock of the terror and fear that we were suffering, the loss of his job and security clearance, he began to concentrate all his efforts to plan a business venture. For the next three years he worked feverishly to plan to own and operate a business. He needed to be sure that he would make a living for his family. And having survived the brutality and ruthlessness of the McCarthy hunt for spies working for the government, he wanted to be prepared with his own business so this would never happen to us again.

This was a critical time for Bern, a time of trial by fire. It was also, because he was so bright and capable, a time of immense productivity and accomplishment for him.. The next decade was one of enormous productivity for both of us, but especially for Bern. In the following three years he was able to put together plans for a business venture to build a bowling alley, to plan all the economic and financial details for the investors, and to supervise the construction. He planned to operate and manage the business himself. This was a gigantic accomplishment. All the while he continued to report to Ft. Monmouth where he was still employed but without a job, and removed to the far-away barracks.

Bern's day began when he went to work in the morning, to the Photo Research Labs. When that work day was over, he would come home for his dinner, and time with his children. And then, at about 9 p.m., he began his other job, as manager of the bowling alleys. He would come home from the bowling alley about 1–2 a.m. He was working long hours daily with two jobs and huge responsibilities. Bern was determined, after our suffering under the brutal victimization of McCarthyism, that he would be financially able to support his family and not be dependent entirely on a government that was willing to sacrifice the lives of its workers as victims for political gain. Bern was very wise and intelligent and he understood fully the constant manipulations that are conducted by politicians and the administration for their own gains to keep themselves in power. He had learned politics and understood how it works from Isaac his wonderful father when he was a young boy. And this is only one instance, although a very important one, in our lives that demonstrated his exceptional and rare qualities as a remarkable man. There were many men who were employed as engineers at Ft. Monmouth who were also persecuted by the horrendous McCarthy witch hunts, in the Army McCarthy hearings. Many did not recover from the onslaught and the victimization and they and their families suffered damage and loss..

For the next twenty years or more we concentrated our efforts on productive and professional work for both Bern and myself, while both children were focused on their education and their careers. Both Jane and Jon were highly motivated and high achieving students. They finished elementary school with honors and high school with honor grades as well. During Jane's junior-senior year, she talked about her great interest in history. Bern's brother in law, Max Blatt, who taught American History in the best high school in NYC for forty years, had stimulated her interest. She wanted to go to summer school at Cornell University for a course in history. We sent her there. Similarly, Jon, who also admired and loved his Uncle Max, and was inspired by him, went to summer school at Columbia University to study anthropology and geology during his junior-senior year. Jane was interested in law, Jon was interested in science and we assumed he would want to continue his interest in medicine. But, at the end of his junior year he began to change his mind. He became interested in being a writer.

In 1947, Albert Camus published his most successful novel, The Plague, a fable of the coming plague to a North African city and its devastating impact on the people's lives. The time and place of this allegory was the time of the German occupation of France in World War II. The story is a fable about good and evil. Camus wrote, "All I can say is that on this earth, there are pestilences (evil) and there are victims." Camus identified the central moral dilemmas of our age as "evil". "The problem of evil will be the fundamental question of life." If we transpose Camus' philosophical allegory to the McCarthy witch hunts looking for spies in the government as 'the plague' that invaded the nation, the McCarthy witch hunts are the evil pestilence. The victims are the innocent government workers. To know about the extent of this plague, the cruelty and barbarism of the McCarthy witch hunts and the effects of this evil on its victims, is to know what an extraordinary man Bern was. He was a survivor.

Bern was an exceptional man, a rare human being. A man unparalleled with an inner landscape of incomparable intelligence and wisdom and deep concern for his family. He was gifted and talented, and sensitive, with a great generosity of heart. Bern had succeeded in his educational and professional life's work in spite of the deafness, the hearing loss in both ears since he was a young boy. And he was passionately in love with his wife and children. For Bern, the cruelest most devastating effect was being pulled out of his job as engineer at the Photo Research Labs (at Ft. Monmouth) and losing his security clearance. And the fear of being unemployable (without security clearance), and not able to support his family. It was as if he was plunged into the depths of hell. It was as if "Hell was spreading all over the world like a drop of ink on blotting paper." (Ceszlaw Milosz) The effect was indescribable. It was the very heart of darkness for Bern, this extraordinary man.

Bern was a man with deep humanitarian concern. He lived a productive life in spite of his deafness. Bern always knew that he would have to overcome his deafness. He was cognizant of how this would affect his life and how he would make this the consideration to provide for his wife and children. Having grown up in the time of the worst economic depression in our history Bern knew of the importance of job security when planning his profession. He knew that it was important to work in a career job with security. Even though after finishing his degrees in engineering he had worked in private industry in two very good jobs and he was offered jobs in private corporations he nevertheless decided to seek employment with the government. He felt that the security of working in Civil Service was the important factor that would ensure that he would be able to support his family. Thus, when he went to work as engineer in the Photo Research Labs at Ft Monmouth a civil service job for the Signal Corps, he was a very happy man. He loved his job and he loved working for the government. He knew that he and his family would be secure. His deafness would not be a problem. He was a loyal government worker.

The analogy to Camus: Bern was a victim of the Army-McCarthy witch hunt along with many other innocent American citizens. They were all victims of "the plague"—the administration's anticommunist crusade. They were the innocent victims of evil that was perpetrated by Joe McCarthy and the FBI under J. Edgar Hoover, whose main goal was to destroy them. McCarthyism was a pestilence, the evil that pervaded the public consciousness. We were the victims along with hundreds of other innocent and loyal American citizens. For the period of Bern's loss of job and security clearance, a period of three years, our life was turned upside down, as if hell was spreading all over.

From the moment that Joe McCarthy and the Army-McCarthy hearings entered Ft. Monmouth; at the same time they appeared on national TV to announce his threats about government employees—as communist spies, Bern knew that he must focus all his strength and ingenuity and responsibility, like his father Isaac, to protect his family. His entire being was focused on taking care of us. He knew that although he had carefully planned his professional career to work for the government because of the security of a job with civil service, he would make more money working in private business. He knew that he must plan to build a business. He could not rely just on security of a civil service job. He knew that he was not safe working in civil service as long as the government employees could be threatened by the politics of an administration obsessed with the a war on communism. He knew that he must have his own business to be secure and not subject to the whims of a Joe McCarthy. In addition, he had always known since he was a young boy that he would live with deafness, hearing loss in both ears, and that he must depend on his own capabilities to have his own business. He did not trust the government. He spent every moment from that day on in planning a business. He planned to build a bowling alley, with a group of investors.

For the next three years he spent all his time, except for his work at the Labs, in researching and working on this plan. We went to many cities to look at bowling alleys, the designs of the building, the trade name of the machines, the way the operations were organized, and the financial arrangements. Bern had thought of every facet to be researched and investigated. He was an extraordinary planner and organizer, he included every detail. Then he prepared a brochure that incorporated every detail of the plan, to present to investors. Bern had superb skills for preparing information for construction and for the operation of business. He was extremely capable in all these fields, and as well in the skills of working with people in an organizational setting. After three years of intensive work he finally completed his plan. He presented the plan to a group of investors and of course it was accepted. He now set about putting the plan into operation. He was ready to buy the property he had picked out (in Eatontown, N.J.), and to arrange for the construction. He planned to supervise the construction himself with sub contractors. He had already researched all the legal aspects himself. Although there was a lawyer on the board Bern knew all the regulations himself.

Bern was a man of extraordinary capabilities as well as intelligence in terms of his knowledge of many fields. When he was a young man he used to take care of his father Isaac's dental lab business. He did the bookkeeping and accounting. When Bern was 17, he would spend every Saturday at Isaac's dental laboratory to do the bookkeeping. He also did the accounting for yearly reports and the taxes. He had read and knew the regulations and the tax laws. And, while he was going to engineering school at CCNY he continued to take care of his father's business. All his life he continued reading about economics and finance both in domestic matters and international, as well. He was smart and knowledgeable and had a quick mind in these matters.

When Bern was still in high school he took the New York State Regents exams for entrance to college. He got a perfect score in English and Math—100 in each. And while he was still in engineering school getting his Master Degree in Mechanical Engineering, he continued to do the accounting for his father Isaac's dental laboratory. Thus he had experience when it was time for him to prepare all the financial, legal and operational material for the bowling alley. He also prepared all the plans for the construction of the building, and for the installation of the equipment, and for the operation of a bar and restaurant as part of the business. He also prepared the detailed financial plans for the investors including the projections for the business and for the profits for the next ten years. The investors were very impressed with his work in operating and managing the business. They knew that they were dealing with a very exceptional man with unique capabilities. Bern's exceptional capabilities were evident to anyone who worked with him. Here was a very special man, a talented man, a man unparalleled in capabilities in his own career, and as well in understanding of the world around us.

These exceptional capabilities were used in his work as Director of Plants and Facilities for the Burlington School Department (Massachusetts), where he worked for thirteen years after we moved to Mass. in 1974. And, the same when he retired from the Burlington School System and went to work as consultant for private companies.

After the McCarthy catastrophe and damaging experience had passed, and McCarthy had died (he died of alcoholism in 1957), and Bern had been returned his security clearance and his job in the Photo Research Labs at Ft Monmouth, we tried to resume some aspects of normal life. After the three and a half years it took to build the bowling alley we settled in to our work. For Bern, it meant working two jobs, round the clock for the next fifteen years. But after the McCarthy horrible years it seemed almost like the ocean returns to a calm and serene body after a raging storm. It was calm to work without fear. And, for Bern it meant that he no longer had to worry about the security of working for the government, and that he would have a way of earning a living to support his family that was not dependent on terrorism and loyalty oath politics of the war scare.

For the next fifteen years, Bern went to work every morning to his job as engineer in the photo research labs at Ft.Monmouth, and came home for dinner and spend time with his family. After one or two hours of rest, he went to work, to manage the bowling alley business, usually until 1 or 2 a.m. in the morning when he would close the business. This was the routine, the work regimen that he set for himself and that he carried out with his strong determination and motivation. He was indeed focused on the determination to provide for his family, and his responsibility to us to take care of us, no matter what it meant for him, in hardship.

Living in the storm of Joe McCarthy's witch hunt hearings was a disaster for us as a family. During the immediate period of the Army-McCarthy witch hunt hearings was a blow especially for Bern. Although there was no outward evidence of his fear, the despair and worry for his family was overwhelming him. As a family we were overcome with fear and worry for each other. Very little conversation took place between us. We were preoccupied with the fear that was gripping us. We felt as if the walls were covered with microphones and that all our thoughts and speech were recorded for the FBI. Our emotions were overcome with dread, and anguish and anxiety. As I watched the ugly predatory figure of Joe McCarthy on the TV screen daily, waving his documents (lists of spies in the government) as he was lurching and screaming and vilifying his victims, I was crying all the time. And when the children came home from school and found me in front of the TV crying, they were filled with fear as well.

At night, Bern and I held on tightly to each other in total fear not knowing what would happen to us. Bern knew that he had to be brave to survive, to see if his job and clearance would be restored. And if he would be able to make a living for his family. I was afraid for Bern that he would not have the strength and determination and will to survive this disastrous set of events. I was afraid knowing that he was so afraid that he would not have a job. But, I knew that I could work as a teacher or specialist in the public schools and that between us we would make a living. Bern was suffering from a multiplicity of fears. One was the fear of surviving in his government job, with the security that this provided, or losing his security and not being able to get another job because he did not have security clearance and he would be unemployable. And the fear of his deafness was always with him and that it would handicap him in getting another job. Bern's self esteem was fragile having lived almost all his life with deafness and knowing that even though for him it was never a problem to succeed, in this case after the McCarthy debacle it could be a problem. We did not know.

As for the children, they seemed to be able to go along every day with their school work with the same enthusiasm and the same exuberance as before. They were always highly motivated, always interested in many things and always good students and high achievers. For the time being we would concentrate on the immediate injury to Bern.

Joe McCarthy intentionally created an atmosphere of terrorism and fear in the public, the fear that there were many government employees whom he could label as "communist" or "spies" who should be fired. The use of terror and fear the intense fear as a method to achieve some political gains was not unknown to us. But, the damage caused by the McCarthy terrorism against many innocent government employees was still a horrible experience for the families to live through.

In the Summer of 1960, there was an article in the local newspaper, The Asbury Park Press, that a group of parents of young deaf children in the county had received approval for their request to start a pilot class for young deaf children in the public school and they were looking for a trained teacher. Since I had a master's degree in Education of the Deaf, and certificate, I was a trained teacher.

I answered the ad, and was interviewed by the parents and hired on the spot by the County Supervisor. The pilot class would be in the basement, an old carpenter shop of an old school building built in 1892, in West Long Branch, N.J. The parents were delighted to find me. I had an M.A. in Education of the Deaf, from Teachers College, Columbia University, and had taught deaf children in both residential schools and in a public school in Ohio. Since New Jersey already had a law requiring the Education of Handicapped Children in the Public Schools, this request only needed approval at the county level. The County Supervisor of Education of Handicapped Children approved the pilot class. She had a list of ten children, all were deaf, and some with other handicapping conditions, ages 4 to 12.

The carpenter's shop in the basement was cleaned out and painted, and chairs and desks were brought in. A very minimum budget was provided, including writing paper pads, and pencils. I ended up buying all other supplies. There was no money for a teacher aide. I realized that this was going to be a difficult job as a single teacher for 10 children, all profoundly deaf, of different ages and with other handicapping conditions. But, I was determined and knew what I had to do to succeed. I discussed this with the parents group, a supportive and helpful group of mothers. We decided that it would be helpful to start a Parent Group for Deaf Children in the county and they would help with whatever I needed to do this job. This was the best arrangement that any teacher could ask for. They offered their help unanimously. We started in September 1960 and the class continued for the next five years until June 1965. It was a most successful program for young deaf children in the public school. They learned to read and write, to understand lip-reading and they made good progress in oral speech. We worked on many experience-type learning projects. I took them for walks to the grocery store a half block from the school almost every day. And then we wrote a daily news story about what we did. Each one learned to write a daily news story. They learned to know each other's names, how to read lips and to write their names, the daily news, i.e., day of the week and the weather. We did a lot of cooking, and wrote about the names of the foods, and what we did with the food. About the school, the bus/or taxi that brought them to school. The children learned language all day—words, names, vocabulary, spelling, sentences. Everything around them and everything they did. I surrounded them with language all day every day. This was the most important goal for me. It was the essence, the core of the curriculum, the educational program for deaf children that they learn—first and foremost, language, reading and writing. It was critical for these children to learn to communicate in language just as normal children do. That is what I knew had to be the same for these young children. Our pilot class was successful beyond everyone's expectations.

Soon word spread around the state among professionals, teachers and administrators, and especially people in special education that this was a very successful program for deaf children in a public school setting. As the word spread we were inundated with requests for visitors from every part of the state. Educators came from many districts to see for themselves what the program was. They wanted to know the curriculum and the methods I was using to teach the deaf children. We had very good support from the local press as well. There were two daily newspapers near us, one in Asbury Park (to the north), and one in Red Bank (to the south). Their best women reporters came to take pictures of the class, the children and the materials that were displayed around the room. They wrote glowing articles about the successful program for deaf children in the public school in their county. And they wrote about the fact that these young children were learning language and reading and writing, so successfully. The parents of course were overjoyed with the success of their children.

The pilot program for young deaf children in the public school setting was clearly successful. It lasted for five years, 1960 to 1965. However, in the spring of 1965 the parents were informed that the program would be discontinued by June. They did not know why or whether their children would be receiving public school education. The parents were devastated. They were worried about the future education of their children. They immediately organized small groups to demonstrate in front of the State Capitol in Trenton, N.J., to let the legislators know about their concerns and the need to continue the education of deaf children in local public school. They demonstrated locally as well in front of the house of the legislator who lived in our county, who was the sponsor of the N.J. Education for Handicapped Children Act. And they wrote numerous letters to the administrator in the office of County Superintendent. But to no avail. The decision had already been made to close the class. We still did not know what would happen to the children.

Later, the parents learned that several teachers in our building, as well as the superintendent in the town had complained to the County Supervisor that they did not want the "deaf children" in their school. They thought it was a hazard, that the deaf children were too "rowdy" and presented a danger to the other children. We learned later that one of the boys in my class, one of the two black children, whose father was in prison, and whose mother was unable to take care of her children, according to the Social Service agency, was eventually shipped off to the State Mental Hospital. They could not find a place for him in the public schools. I also learned that one of my children, a young boy who was deaf and blind, and very bright, and who had made exceptional progress in learning to read and write, had been accepted in a residential school in another state. According to his mother he was continuing to do very well. He was "blossoming" as a result of the progress he made in my class. Another young boy was accepted in the State School for the Deaf to continue his education and vocational training. This was on the basis that he had shown good learning ability in my class. I don't know what happened to the other children.

By this time, I was known in the county as a very good teacher/educator, as a teacher of deaf children and also for my work in developing curriculum for children with language, speech and reading difficulties. In the summer of 1965 I received a call from the Superintendent of Schools in Tinton Falls. He (George Malone) said, "Hello Clara, I need a Speech Therapist for my school district." He asked me to come in to see him. I went the next day and was hired. This was another beginning for me. It was another milestone in my career which eventually led me to receive a doctorate degree (Ed.D.) with specialization in psycholinguistics—the study of language development in children. I became a specialist in evaluating children with language and reading and writing disabilities, i.e., dyslexia. I have done hundreds of evaluations of children with dyslexia, in reading and writing. As a specialist I have testified in many cases of children with language/reading disabilities at administrative hearings in Special Education. I have worked closely with the attorneys who represented these children, and with my expertise and my expert evaluations we have won many cases. The children we represented all received appropriate remediation programs.

Bern Made It All Possible. All of my years of work and success in a career was made possible by Bern's complete and enduring support at every step of the way. His deep love was like a cradle of nourishment and encouragement and a constant support. He made things possible, he always let me know that he had confidence in me and that he knew I would be successful. With his intuitive and caring nature he was always perceptive and figured out what had to be done to make it possible for me to work. He always was a step ahead to help me make the decisions I had to make and to take care of the details, whether financial or other details that were needed. It was as though with his exceptional wisdom he was clearing the path for me to proceed successfully. With his inexhaustible nurturing and caring he made things possible for me to have a successful career. It was the only way it could have happened for me.

These were the productive years for both of us. This was the time when Bern's dream of having a family that he loved passionately and was able to support in the way his father had supported his family came to be realized. He was able to work, and to have a successful business and to support us and guide us as his father had done for him. We loved each other, we appreciated and cared for each other and our children. It was as if our struggle through the horrific troubled times (of McCarthyism) was over and we were able to survive. As Chekhov once said, "Life is given to us only once". We lived through it.

Clara Maslow, Professor of Education, Castleton College, Vt., 1975

7

WOUNDS THAT WILL NOT HEAL

It has long been accepted wisdom that "each of us is the child of our times" But there are few people who know the origin of this bit of wisdom. It was a thoroughly novel idea when Hegel expressed it in his writing in 1821. It implied then as it does now that human nature is not a timeless essence, a blank, but is in fact penetrated through and through by our historical situation. Our nature, our character, our personal relationships are each a metaphor of our landscape of beliefs and attitudes and feelings toward other human beings. We are strongly influenced and our conscience imprinted by our own experiences of time, place and events. In our case, Bern, myself and our two children were caught in the crucible of terror and fear of McCarthyism, in the hearing at Ft. Monmouth. This historical event clearly influenced and shaped out experience and affected our own relationships, as it did our children's.

Our two children, Jane and Jonathan were born and raised in a warm, loving relationship. They were a true example of tabula rasa, a wall of love without fear or insecurity it was the essence of out family relationship and our trust. Security and safety were the essence of Bern's caring love for us what he had envisioned long ago when he was growing up with Isaac, as mentor. He inherently felt responsibility for those he loved, to take care of them. And, when he thought about a profession and career, his first thought was to take care of, to provide, to secure, to ensure the safety of and to make a living. That was the essence of his character, his person, his life, his reason for being. This is what made him so remarkable, so exceptional a human being. That is, until this very essence of his character was blown up in the nightmare of the Army-McCarthy hearings, and the deliberate state of a Red Scare in the Cold War of the Truman Administration.

There is no doubt that the McCarthy witch hunt caused Bern's difficulty, that Bern's loss of security clearance and job displacement affected us. It frightened us. We felt victimized and punished. These frightening events put an unbearable strain on our relationship on each one of us. It challenged our daily lives our existence and eventually caused the connecting wires of our loving relationship to break. We felt the effects of the trauma differently. Historical events tend to create in the individual a transformation of the hurt and injured feelings into contending images and myths. In our experience the fear created anger and insecurity of huge proportions. So great was the pressure from the fear and insecurity of these events, so painful the feelings, that the effect remained hidden for several years before it surfaced. Like an underground raging current.

We were victims caught in the horrendous tidal wave of the McCarthy assault on innocent citizens and we were literally almost drowned by the effect of the savagery of these persecutions. Our lives were insignificant and worthless in the grand scheme of the McCarthy terrorism scare, and the scare of anticommunism of the government. We were sunk in a pit of terror and fear. For months we remained huddled in our house, Bern and I and our two children. There was no communication with the outside world around us as the Army-McCarthy hearings progressed for several weeks/months. No one used the phone, no calls came in, no calls went out to friends or family. Everyone who had any connection to Ft. Monmouth knew that our phones were tapped. Everyone knew that the FBI was circulating around the entire area and had been visiting neighbors for the past year. It was truly like a reign of terror that we were living through.

Our first fear was for the children, Jane and Jon. My fear was for Bern. I knew that this was an unbearable, insufferable blow. I did not know whether he would survive. I knew it would take remarkable strength and courage, and determination, and almost inhuman strength of character to get us out of this black hole. The monsters had wounded and almost killed Bern. We did not know the extent of the damage to our family. The fear and pain are indescribable, and the worry for us as a family was central.

The fear and pain and worry eventually were displaced with work and striving to help Bern build a business, and to make a living for his family. I was busy with starting a teaching career and the children were busy achieving in their school.

But the seeds of the fear and paranoia which arose with the McCarthy events continued to burn under the surface and to eventually cause strains in our loving relationships. And, eventually to rupture our relationship with both our children to the extent that, since 1996, when Jane sent Bern her hateful and angry letter. The letter to "Dear Dad" dated Jan. 1996 said, "Clara and Bernie treat their dogs like children and their children like dogs."

This shocking and hurtful letter was like a bolt of lightening striking the heart for Bern especially. To Bern it was so devastating that he became depressed and he could not speak for months. It was more than he could bear and more than his own identity as a loving father could cope with. After having lived through and survived the psychological damage of the McCarthy events, this was too much for him to bear. For months he remained very quiet, unable to make sense of this anger (and hate) from his loving daughter. He thought that he was to blame for working too many hours and not spending enough time with the children. Also he thought that he should have been more involved in their upbringing and in providing more guidance, more discussion about our values. He thought that he could have been more involved in disciplining our children. Our children seemed to have lost their way, the loving child-parent relationship was gone. They seemed to be confused. They seemed to have their wires crossed and misunderstandings carried over into their own personal relationships as well. Both had numerous problems in their own relationships while growing up, in making decisions about marrying. Both went through several stormy relationships with partners. But, we were not prepared for the anger and misinterpretations that came through in the text of this letter. Bern began his descent into total despair, which continued until his untimely death. Jane never called to say "I'm sorry. I made a mistake, I still love you." She never came to give us a hug, to say "I love you." She does not know how to do these simple things to demonstrate her love. Behavior that is so normal between parents and their children.

Jane, our first born, was a beautiful little girl and bright as a button, with a sparkling personality, warm and loving. She was excited and interested in everything in the stories we read, the songs we sang, the flowers in the woods and all the animals. She especially loved dogs and by the time she was twelve she had saved up twenty five dollars for a dog. She had researched The Dog Life magazine to find the right breed of dog she wanted. Watching her grow and listening to her eloquent speech and adult language use as a toddler was a happy experience for us. She was a loving child with lots of talents and endless creativity in every project she did. She was exceptional and special to us. She was unusually bright and thoughtful in many ways like Bern. She adored Bern, with idyllic devotion as if he was a god. She was sensitive to Bern's every word, every motion, every look. Through the early years when she was growing up she was so attached to Bern that it seemed almost that she had no need for me. But, of course she was close to me. We went everywhere together as a family. We visited friends, and family, we went on vacations, we attended museums, and concerts. We were always together as a loving family.

As Jane grew up to be a pre-teen and then adolescent she remained fixated with Bern, and still looked up to him as her primary parent-model. She discussed everything with him, he was her mentor, still her God. She even kept secrets about some things with him while I was left out. But since Bern was already working round the clock, in two jobs, and I was working, as teacher of a pilot class of young deaf children in the public school, we were busy and did not think of this favoritism as a problem. It seemed normal. We were so happy with our children that it would never occur to Bern or to me to think that this could be a dark cloud to be watched. Our children were so loving, so perfect.

By the time Jane was 18 years old, and ready to graduate to college, she was an independent person and we thought she was mature. She was an excellent student with high achievements. She had always been an honor student, she knew how to study and always achieved high marks. She had attended Cornell Summer School in between her sophomore and junior year in high school. And she had attended Princeton University during her junior year in college, as an exchange student, to study Chinese history. She was an accomplished young woman. We were very proud. And every summer for about ten years, as they were growing up, Jane and Jon attended a wonderful progressive summer camp where they met with other interesting young people and continued these friendships.

During the school year Jane was immersed in her homework, and since she was away every summer, for the entire summer, she had little time to spend with me. When her Dad, Bern, asked her to help me with the chores like helping with the dishes after dinner, she always had an excuse, "I have too much homework." Neither Bern nor I ever insisted that she help. After the unfortunate harsh letter to Bern (of January 1996), he began to think reflectively and realized that he should have insisted when she was growing up that she be responsible for helping with some chores, and that she should learn to be more responsible in general as a family member. But, of course it was too late, and we both realized this. We also realized after much introspection that our wonderful child, Jane, was a very mixed up individual. She had many crossed wires in her interpretation of our values, and our ideas, and along the way she had misinterpreted almost everything. It was clear to us that she had mixed her priorities. For one thing she had put achievement in her school work at the top of her values, over showing her love for parents, for her brother, or for her step-children. Her life was always frantic, trying to raise her accomplishment and be outstanding in her work. The effect was to neglect all other action. It seems that in her relationships over the years the values that suffered most from this obsession with achievement was spending time and effort to show how you care for the ones you say you love. In talking to our granddaughter Emily (Jane's daughter) and to Paul's three children (from his previous marriage) we have heard the same story. The children all felt that her life was always in "chaos" and that she neglected them. They felt abandoned by her. Her life is obsessed with her work, her achievements (as a Law Professor).

The estrangement from me, which began when she was about twelve did not register in my consciousness until a few years later. Bern and I were busy working round the clock in our multiple jobs. I assumed that the fact that she did not talk to me very much was because she was really busy with school work. Also, I thought this was part of normal development and growing up. It was when the alienation reached a critical point that I began to think of it as a real problem, a mother-daughter problem. It became so troubling to me that I decided to seek counseling help. I needed to understand this in the context of our relationship, our family relationship and what had happened to us in the McCarthy horrible period living with fear and paranoia. How did the trauma of the horrendous McCarthy persecutions affect our relationships? How had these fearful events affected our children. And how did these traumatic events produce the psychological damage of crossed wires and misinterpretations that followed? I sought counseling for several years. I needed to know how and why these problems occurred in our family.

Jane spent her junior college year at Princeton University to study Chinese language and history. She was a history major at Wellesley. At Princeton, she met a very lively group of young men, and even brought five of them home for Thanksgiving dinner in the fall. At the end of the year, in June, she came home to let me know that she was packing up her belongings to move. She was going back to finish school at Wellesley and then to live in Cambridge. The tone of her voice was angry and final. This was not a simple statement. There was much more that was not stated. And when I questioned her for some explanation since we had not discussed the decision either between ourselves or with Bern I received a cold, short answer which led to an argument between the two of us. This brought out the real anger and hatred. It ended up in an angry encounter. This left me not just hurt, but perplexed. I had not heard a word of this from Bern and I did not know whether she had talked to him without me, and left me out intentionally. The suddenness and the seriousness of the decision led to the argument. Jane was 18 years old at the time it was the first serious talk that we ever had and it was the first time that our relationship was challenged. The hurt feelings were shocking and painful to me. I'm sure to both of us. For me it was a terrible feeling of being alone of losing my child, a part of my life that I loved and cherished. I was worried.

From that time on until now Jane, my only daughter, and I have had no relationship no close contact of any kind. Practically no communication. We have greeted each other when we visited her or when she came for dinner to our house but it was a cold wind that passed between us. There was an absence of love and warmth and embrace that usually passes between mother and child. There seems to be an avoidance of feelings. Instead, as she sat in our kitchen numerous times I could feel the watchfulness, the suspicion and the criticism. It was touchable. And all through the years there has been the veiled suspicion and criticism the feeling that she cannot come close to me to talk to me but (must) sit across the street on the curb and throw stones like a little girl. It is like her own Intifada. She has built a wall, a cage around herself and has refused to come out to see me, to know me, to know who I am. To acknowledge that I am her mother.

Bern was never aware that Jane and I had a bad relationship. He was always involved in his work in trying to provide for us in every way. It never occurred to him that Mother and daughter were in difficulty. It would never occur to him to think in such terms. And, of course it would never occur to him to relate this poor relationship to the effects of the horror and trauma of McCarthy witch hunts. It was not until the December 1995 incident at dinner at our house with Jane and Larry, her second husband and the fateful and hurtful letter of January 1996, to "Dear Dad", that he had any knowledge of the difficulties in our relationship with Jane. We also learned from the letter that she had purposefully kept Emily, our grandchild, away from us while she was growing up for over twenty years. We also did not know of the effects on Emily of this deliberate separation from us. And we did not know of the anger and hateful feelings that Jane had carried within herself against us for all these years. We knew that we had longed to bond with our grandchild Emily, and that we had never had the pleasure of having her visit us when she was small so that we could enjoy her. We loved our granddaughter, we needed her, to be with her as she was growing up.

Bern was so devastated by this letter and the realization that Jane spent most of her life holding on to her insecurity and her paranoia and turning these anxieties into hatred. He went into deep depression for many months. He lived with despair all the time. He continued to remark that his children had "no respect for us," that our children had no appreciation of our struggle against the horrendous experience of McCarthyism, and our commitment to them in spite of these hardships. It would seem that they must have been so disturbed by the traumatic effects of psychological fear during the McCarthy hearings, that their feelings became disoriented. Bern and I discussed many times the fact that our children had such difficulty in showing their love for us.

Jane graduated from Wellesley in 1967 and she was admitted to Yale Law School. Paul, her history professor had separated from his wife. They were divorced and he was given custody of their three young children. Jane and Paul married. They lived in Cambridge together with Paul's young children, while she commuted from Boston to New Haven, Connecticut to attend Law School. In 1970, Emily was born, our only grandchild. Soon they bought a large house in Lincoln, a wealthy suburb. The family was Jane and Paul and their four children.

When Emily was five, Jane left Paul. She picked up Emily and moved to a rented house in Cambridge. This happened shortly after a Thanksgiving holiday in which we had come up to visit them. Not a word was mentioned about the intended separation and move during our visit. We learned about the move only later after we were home in New Jersey. The years following this separation and divorce from Paul, and Jane's life after her divorce is almost a closed book to us, She had affairs with several other men. Jane never called us to discuss or explain the important events of her life she seldom came to visit us, she was busy establishing her career as a law professor. And, never brought our granddaughter Emily to visit us or stay for a weekend, or holiday. We did not know why. We felt alienated and cut off, but did not question her. We had always had such complete confidence in our children in their intelligence and judgment and ability to make their own decisions, wisely, that we felt we had to respect their wish for privacy. And so, in all the years of silence, we never knew why, after such a stormy fight to marry Paul, she would suddenly decide that she did not love him and would abruptly end the marriage. We also were quietly resigned to the fact that we did not have any relationship with our granddaughter, and that we had never had an opportunity to bond with her. This realization was particularly sensitive for Bern. Given his own wonderful relationship with his parents, especially with his father he could not understand this hostility and alienation. The fact is that he felt so close, so bonded in his relationship with his own children. This was a subject so delicate for him that I seldom mentioned it, not wanting to hurt his feelings. He was a very sensitive man, and he was passionate in his feelings for his family. For many years we lived quietly with the feeling of loss of our relationship with Emily. But, we felt that there was little we could do, it was in Jane's hands, and evidently this is the way she wanted it. We did not know why.

In December 1995, when Emily was 25, she began to visit with us regularly. We began to see each other to get to know each other and to have a relationship. We discovered that she had wanted a family all her life, when growing up, wanted to know about us, but was never told about us. She just hoped that she would someday know us and love us. For the next few years, Bern and I made every opportunity to visit with her and to have her visit with us. It was wonderful for us to finally have a relationship with our granddaughter who was an exceptional warm loving individual.

She has expressed her joy in finally knowing us, and knowing all about our lives, and our families. She was delighted to know what exceptional and interesting people were included in our families. And knowing that she could trace her own character and talents to us, and to our parents. She is hungry for every story that I tell her about when Bern was a little boy and growing up with Isaac, and as well about the individual family members who lived in Russia and their personalities and their exceptional talents and creativity. Emily was with me in the hospital when Bern died; a wrongful death. She knows now that Bern was an exceptional, a remarkable man, and she is happy that she was able to know him. She did know how exceptionally wonderful he was, as a man, as her grandfather.

Emily and I now have a close bonded relationship, in which there is complete admiration, trust and love for each other. She has lived with me three days a week for almost a year. In that time we have come to know each other. I think she is a most exceptional young woman, intelligent and thoughtful, considerate and generous and very much like Bern and me. She has learned about Bern, and what a remarkable man he was. And, recently she expressed the thought that she wants to find a husband like Bern, and like her father, Paul. Even though she knows that these two men in her life were exceptional and it means setting a high standard the more she knows about Bern, the more she loves him. She has the same feelings about her father. And as for me, she feels that having lived with me this past year, and knowing me at close range, she realizes how secure and safe she is with me and how I love her. And, she knows now how important we are to her and how much she needed us in her life when she was growing up.

Emily has been trying for the past year since Bern died to bring us together, Jane and me for reconciliation, and as a means to resolving some of her own difficult problems with her mother. Thus far, Jane has been resistant. She continues to repeat her feelings of me as a "monster", someone who caused her to alienate herself from her parents. But, what Jane does not say is that she has built up a huge myth about us and that she misinterpreted everything we said so that she finally ended up with a mass of crossed wires in our relationship. It had the effect of building a cage around herself, with misinterpretations and myth, where no one can enter, and she is not willing, or too fearful and insecure to unravel these myths. As a result she holds on to these myths. It is now evident to Emily and she feels that it has interfered with her own mother-daughter relationship. Emily also understands how hurtful this alienation was for Bern. And especially hurtful when she expressed it as "Clara and Bernie treat their dogs like children and their children like dogs." Knowing Bern now as she does she knows that he was in deep despair because of this hate letter. And that he died in deep despair.

When Jonathan was a junior in high school, he came home one day through the back door into the kitchen and smiled—he had shaved his head. He did not have an explanation except to say that he did it impulsively. Bern and I were seriously worried. Knowing what a happy child he had always been, what could possibly be wrong, or what was bothering him?

Jonathan was born smiling. He was a beautiful little baby. As a little boy he was always happy and smiling, he loved everyone and everything, and everyone loved him. As a little boy he never walked he always skipped. He was always in a good humor and made jokes about everything. He seemed never to have a worry, everything always seemed good in his world. He was a happy-go-lucky personality. He was always an excellent student, he was always on the honor roll and his teachers always loved him. What could be bothering him now? It was more than ten years after the McCarthy witch hunt that nearly destroyed his loving dad and our family.

In addition, he told me that he had changed his mind about wanting to be a doctor. It was our impression that he always wanted to be a doctor. Why a change of direction now? He explained it by saying that he finally realized that he "could not stand the site of blood." Bern and I were worried. Knowing our son Jon, and his outward personality we felt that we needed help. We convinced Jon to go for counseling. Jon agreed, as he usually did, and he went to see a psychologist. He came back after a few visits; "he was o.k."

But, to me, intuitively as his mother, it was still disturbing. I felt we did not know the whole reason. I thought of the past ten years under the psychological trauma of the McCarthy hearings that we went through. I thought that possibly the seeds of fear and paranoia were beginning to sprout. Could it be that what Bern suffered during the traumatic period of McCarthyism had made its mark on the consciousness of our children? And that, this insecurity and paranoia was the basis of their confused thinking and behavior? I sensed that we must be watchful to see how this insecurity and paranoia would become evident. I know that Bern was thinking along these same lines. Bern was a very observant and sensitive parent he knew that we had lived through the trauma and suffering of the horrendous McCarthy assault on our family. He was deeply concerned about Jonathan's behavior. And so for the next few years we watched.

Jon finished high school with honor grades and went on to Wesleyan University, the college of his choice. After one semester he complained to Bern that he was not happy at this school. There were too many students who spent weekends just bombed out on drugs. He wanted to move to a small college in Vermont, Marlboro College. We did not question his decision and he made the transfer. Bern gave him a new car, a Volvo, so that he would have safe transportation. For the next three years he lived in an old farmhouse in the woods outside of Marlboro with no running water, no heat, and no windows. Heat was provided by a wood stove in the kitchen. Jon parked his new Volvo car in the deep woods on a bed of leaves soaked by rain and snow for the entire winter. Naturally, the whole underside of the car was rusted out. Jon and two other students lived in this utter ramshackle house for two years. He said that he did not need money. They lived on root vegetables which were cheap like winter squash, etc. He bought his clothes at the Salvation Army second hand store. This was his life style his way of life for the next several years.

The Salvation Army clothes was a metaphor for Jon's life style for the next twenty years, a rebellion against materialism, against owning material goods, and against working for the government, or an institution (from which he could be fired). He wanted to prove that he could live free and achieve in a career but not have to go through the terrible ordeal that his father went through. He was going to show the world that he wanted to work but be free of the institutions that can victimize its workers.

Meanwhile, he brought the new Volvo car home with the chassis completely rusted out. We put it out on the driveway and sold it for $250. He also decided that he wanted to take time off from school. He wanted to move to New York City, to live and work as a free lance writer. He thought that he would be able to sell an article or two, to support himself, while learning how to write. All this sounded childish to us. We thought maybe some day soon he would outgrow this immaturity. He moved to NYC.

For the next ten years or more Jonathan traveled to many places mainly Central and South America and wrote many articles and two books. But we did not know what his goals were. He was not clear in discussing these goals with us. He seemed to be ever elusive. In 1973, during the chaotic events in Chile when there was a CIA-inspired coup, the dictator Augusto Pinochet came to power for the next twenty five years. A group of young American journalists had gone there. Jon was there at the time as a free lance journalist. He left Chile just in the nick of time as the coup was starting. We were happy to see him come home alive. He came home to New Jersey to a buy a house in Cape May County. He did not have a job but was still doing free-lance writing. Although, in this period he had his first book published. It was the Owl Book, in collaboration with Leonard Baskin, the artist-sculptor who was Bern's cousin. Leonard Baskin was the son of Rabbi Samuel Baskin, who was the brother of Lisa, Bern's mother. Jon wrote the narrative and Leonard made the illustrations for the Owl Book. It was a beautiful edition and sold well. Unfortunately in the financial contract, Jon did not provide or take care of his interest and so did not profit from the sales. The Owl Papers has been out of print for many years. Since then Jon has written another book, the title is Bird of Life, Bird of Death, a Naturalist's Journey Through A Land of Political Turmoil. It is about his journey to Guatemala to observe the Quetzal bird, the seriously endangered species because of the loss of its habitat. In the course of his journey he describes the human and natural landscape of Guatemala, one of the most repressive countries in the Western Hemisphere. This was published in 1986.

Jon had a friend teaching at Louisiana State University. Through this friend Jon landed a job teaching journalism at the university. He taught a course in environmental journalism each semester. While teaching there he lived with a woman divorcee, with a young daughter. During this time we were told that he had met a very special woman named Sara who was an editor at Rolling Stone magazine, published in California. They had met in California. She was now living in New York and had become an independent agent and publisher. They decided to get married and were married in Mexico. They came home to introduce us to our new daughter in law. We were very happy for Jon and very impressed with Sara. She was an exceptional woman, warm, loving, intelligent and pretty. From the minute we met her we felt that Sara was part of our family. Sara came from Pennsylvania, her father was a dentist. When Sara and Jon came home her parents made a huge party for our families to meet. We all traveled to Pennsylvania for the party. We were housed in a beautiful motel, where we were wined and dined on the best of everything.

Sara moved into Jon's house in Dennisville, N.J., although she maintained her apartment in NYC for her business. She commuted to her office Monday through Wednesday. She was at home Thursday through Sunday. They seemed very happy. They had much in common both being in the field of journalism. Sara had many contacts in the publishing business, she introduced Jon to his agent and publisher at Random House. Soon they let us know that Sara was pregnant. And, in the next month they let us know they learned that the fetus was malformed. Her doctor recommended to abort. Not long afterward Sara was pregnant again.

When Sara was pregnant in the second month she discovered that she had a lump in her breast. She sought out the best doctors at Sloan-Kettering Institute Medical Center. They advised her that she could have a lumpectomy procedure instead of a complete mastectomy. She chose the lumpectomy. But also they would have the fetus aborted because of the cancer. In the course of these consultations with the specialists at Sloan Kettering and the difficult decision to make about the proper procedure, Jon was behaving badly. He seemed to be angry all the time. At the time, he was independently researching about the procedures in the medical journals in the library. Then he would visit with Sara in the hospital and argue with her. He created a terrible disturbance, making a spectacle of himself with his outrageous behavior. This was not like a rational, reasonable, caring husband. It was more like a child with an uncontrolled temper. We were worried about him.

We were disheartened with his childish behavior, but more worried with his lack of consideration for Sara in her condition, knowing that she needed more loving support and care instead of this display of anger.. We both knew that Jon's inappropriate behavior at this critical time was wrong and damaging. We also knew that it had become part of a pattern of behavior with him when he felt threatened and insecure. We were convinced that this exhibition of temper tantrum was his response to the trauma effect of fear in McCarthyism. We recognized the symptoms. He was having difficulty coping with their medical problems. The situation was threatening and he did not know how to cope with the seriousness of it, and the fact that it concerned the two lives that were important to him. We did not know how to help him. And we were sorry for Sara. We knew that he would not go for psychiatric help, but that he would continue to 'blame' her. Jon had refused help when he was younger when it would have helped him. Now we felt resigned that it was too late. We felt very sorry for our loving son Jonathan.

We learned several years later that during this time when Sara and Jon were going through the misfortune with her breast cancer, that he was teaching his course in Louisiana and, that he was having an affair with a woman there. This was another blow to us, to Bern in particular. It was almost more than he could bear. He was by now so disappointed in Jon, as well as in Jane. And he felt so defeated that all his effort and work to survive the McCarthy witch hunt would result in this ultimate damage to our children.

After Sara recovered from the cancer operation she was anxious to go on with their life together. But Jon seemed no longer connected. His attention had wandered. They ended by getting divorced. We learned later that Sara did not want a divorce. She still loved Jonathan. A few months later he came to visit us to tell us he had met an exciting woman in Mississippi, when he was working there on a writing project. She was a journalist, her family owned and published a newspaper there. He said she was beautiful, she rode horses, which her family owned. They were planning to get married. He was taking riding lessons to be able to ride with her.

A few months later Jon told us that he was all set to go to Mississippi to get married. We made note of the date. About a week after the date of the wedding we received a call from him. A troubled call. He had been married and after a few days he had to leave. She filed for divorce. Once more he was distressed and again was blaming her. All that we could learn was that after two days he lost his temper, he had a temper tantrum. This time he said, on his own, that he was going to see a psychologist. He went for a few visits (like he did when he was in high school) and the psychologist agreed with him. It was her fault.

By this time we knew that Jon had some difficult and long-standing problems. We had been over this history of temper tantrums and heated conversations before when he was in difficulty and trying to cope with his situation. We knew that this was beyond his control. He could not control his temper tantrums. They sprang up so instantly when he found himself in a tight spot in a situation where it appeared that he might have made a mistake. He could not accept this failure, or more likely the weakness in himself. We understood the situation. Once more we thought of the long term effects of the fear and paranoia during the McCarthy witch hunt. Our two children had not escaped the terribleness of the McCarthy persecution that had victimized Bern. We realized that our two children had been affected over the long term by the psychological fear, and paranoia. Both were suffering the effects but in different ways.

Jonathan is now married for the third time. This time to a woman who is a Russian immigrant who came over to the US with her family, a husband and a son and her mother and grandmother. They came to the U.S. with a large number of Russian immigrants during the seventies. Jon met this woman on the subway. He wrote to Bern, to explain that she appealed to him because she was not like the others (American women) he had married. She would not 'argue' with him. He knew she was the right woman because, "the Russian women are submissive. They do not argue with their husbands. They do not disagree with their husbands." Jon and Liliya have lived together now for over twenty years. We do not know whether he still exhibits the temper tantrums, like before.

What happened to our two beautiful and bright young children in the horrible climate of terror and fear instituted by the McCarthy persecutions and the Truman Administration in the Cold War? We raised our children with such love, as caring parents in such a happy secure home in such a safe and friendly community as The Vail Homes. Yet, the McCarthy witch hunt created a frightening climate of fear and insecurity that seeped through all of us? Our loving relationship with our children was sacrificed. It was blown against the rocks in the horrid sea of McCarthyism.

Our two loving children who spent their early years listening to music, singing songs and rhymes, reading stories and playing games, engulfed in happy interesting cultural activities in the wonderfully rich environment of The Vail Homes have suffered the long term effects of the trauma of psychological fear and paranoia that we as a family experienced in the crucible of McCarthyism.

How did the terrible fear and insecurity, manage to affect the strong web of bonding of love between us? How did this fear and paranoia infect our loving relationship? It is difficult to describe the furor, the ferocity of the McCarthy psychological terrorism attacks on us as a family, and on each one individually. We were victims caught in the historical events. Bern's first and immediate response was to plan for making a living for his family, since he did not trust what the government would do with regard to his security clearance. My immediate thought was to help Bern survive this violence against his person. And then to keep the children from being hurt. To protect them with love and devotion in order to not interfere with their natural motivation in school. We thought we were able to keep this destructive emotional blow from affecting the children. We thought we had emerged from the worst imaginable and horrendous emotional fear of our lives. We were not prepared to see the effects of this horrendous upheaval surface in our children's lives.

I have described the difficulties in growing up with Jane, and her problems with her first marriage, and with Emily, our granddaughter. And the rough road of Jon's growing up with his two mistakes in marriage until he settled down in his muddled way. But, it was in our personal relationship with each one that we had the worst effect. It was as if we were always talking with them in crossed wires. It was as if they seemed to misinterpret what we said every time we had a discussion. Instead of coming back to indicate they understood or had a different opinion, it seemed to cause more strain in the relationship. We were increasingly alienated as the years went by. Their lives reflect their insecurity in their own relationships. But with us each one developed their own cage of their own reality. It was difficult and it was often discouraging for us as parents to see the effects of the misinterpretations. It was difficult to face the fact that our children had great trouble in showing their love for us in expressing words of love to us. I don't remember ever having heard Jane say "I love you" either to her dad or to me. I know she never gave me a hug. She has avoided all human contact. Only her linguistic skills to make contact.

Neither Jane nor Jon, although with superior intelligence and professional accomplishment, ever wanted to discuss with us the horrendous family experience with McCarthy and the witch hunt hearings and persecution of their father. We don't know what they think. And we don't know what they understand of the effects of those horrendous times on Bern. I don't believe they know the full extent of Bern's suffering of the attack against his own confidence and personality and the fact that he was almost fatally shattered. They do not know that he suffered from the lingering paranoia the rest of his life. (As Victor Navasky, The Nation Editor, said, "The paranoia lingers on.")

For Bern, it was the real heart of darkness, it was the worst of times. It was a shock to his ego, his love for his wife and children. It robbed him of self confidence and the ability to provide for his family and security for his children. This was his life, a daily struggle to survive, to overcome the fear and insecurity and paranoia that was gripping him every moment. I watched him closely over the years under this severe strain to fight to achieve his goals to provide for us. He fought with all his strength daily to overcome the demons of fear and paranoia. He was a remarkable man, an exceptional human being, to be able to overcome the strain of these events. And to achieve as he did. He was a man unparalleled in strength, an inner landscape of wisdom, great intellect and intense love for his wife and children. This was a man, a jewel among men, who overcame the victimization of the horrendous McCarthy persecutions. And, finally after years of such struggle to come out of the darkness and hell only to face our loving children who have inherited the fear and paranoia that they are unable to return the passionate love we have given them all their lives.

Bern died a wrongful death, an untimely death. He had been in deep despair due to the alienation of our two wonderful children. He felt that in spite of his passionate love for his family that our children did not feel respect for us. They never came to tell Dad how much they loved him, how much they respected him. They never came to show us how they loved us. Never called to say, "I love you Mom, I love you Dad." They have no respect.

8

OUR TWO CHILDREN; TWO PERSONALITIES

You have navigated with raging soul far from the paternal
home, passing beyond the sea's double rocks, and you
now inhabit a foreign land. Medea.

What happened to our two bright and beautiful children? When and how did
our close loving relationship become twisted, like crossed wires in a blinding
storm, and how did our relationship end up on the sea's double rocks, in the sea
of misunderstandings and misinterpretations? With love so disoriented? In the
early years, the happiest, the best of times, we were living in the Vail Homes that
wonderful joyous community with our two beautiful bright children. Bern was a
civilian engineer, Assistant Director of the Photographic Labs, life was happy and
filled with love. Until Senator Joe McCarthy appeared in 1954 at Ft. Monmouth,
for his witch hunt hearings the continuation of the cold war/anticommunist
crusade. Bern was pulled out of his job, he loved, and his security removed so that
he became unemployable. Our loving family was thrown into a state of terror,
fear and panic. Along with the other families affected, as was the nation. We were
devastated, practically destroyed.

That horrendous historical event instantly changed our family drastically from
the happiest days of our lives to one of the heart of darkness, insecurity and the
fury of fear. As the children grew, our relationships were affected adversely by the
effects of the fear and insecurity. It was a path of crossed wires, misinterpretations
disoriented love, and relationships on the rocks. After the initial shock, and
terror, our relationship turned from one of love and affection, devotion and
caring, to the later adult relationship of alienation, self involvement, self

92

protection, insulation, disrespect. Our children's ability to show love and affection seemed to have melted away, washed into the sea of fear.

In the early years our family life was a landscape of love and devotion, of father, mother, a steady, secure job. Bern had a great job as an engineer in photographic research at Ft. Monmouth. He was well respected, well-liked by everyone, both civilians and military personnel. He was hard working, productive, and a great administrator, at work. In terms of work, Bern and I inherited our work ethics from our European-born parents that incorporated workaholic habits, intellect and freedom of thought. To understand the events, the passions and truths of our conflicted lives, one must see the connections between the landscape of the repressive historical events of the fear and our individual characters and personalities. Each one internalized the psychological fear and terror of McCarthyism in their own individual ways.

And then, there are individual differences in how each of our children internalized the terror and fear that descended on us. Our secure and happy landscape was transformed into a landscape of lingering fear, insecurity, hurtful relationships for many years.

Janie, our first born was a beautiful, especially bright, happy little girl with blonde hair and green eyes. She had a sparkling personality, curious and inventive, an absorbing mind like a sponge and a glittering sense of humor, like her Dad, Bern. She was astute, perceptive, and literally absorbed knowledge like a sponge. She was an early reader, about age 3 and a delight for every teacher all through elementary and high school. She always knew her assignments, always turned in exceptional written papers which she spent hours into the night preparing.

She loved animals, particularly horses. I took her for weekly riding lessons in which she was outstanding; she won several prizes. She also made many drawings of horses. We have a prize winning drawing of horses made in the sixth grade. It is unmistakable talent.

Jane also loved dogs. When she was 8 she decided she wanted a dog. She subscribed to the journal Dog World, to read about the different breeds, their nature and personalities. Finally she decided she wanted an Airedale. We spent the next few months, every week end, driving from farm to farm, to every state to find the right Airedale. We bought a puppy, Janie named him Brandy. She (and I) enrolled in training lessons. The training was not successful, the dog needed more training at home. One day Brandy ran out of the house across the road and was hit by a car.

Then it was Jonathan's turn to choose a dog. After again visiting breeders, he picked another Airedale. We had this dog about seven years, and again, he was hit by a car and passed on.

Janie was an exceptional child, talented and gifted, listening to her eloquent speech her wonderful innate use of language as a little girl was a delight. She was admired by friends, teachers, other children. Bern especially was proud since he was an eloquent speaker with a wonderful use of language. Janie adored her father (like most little girls do), he was her model, her mentor. She was sensitive to his every word, every look, every expression. She wanted to be an intellectual, a professional, to speak and write like her dad.

About the age of thirteen, as Jane was growing into adolescence, she began to withdraw from her relationship with me. This was about five years after the immediate traumatic effects of the McCarthy witch hunt, the Ft. Monmouth firings, the terror and fear that settled on the community, on us, and what happened to Bern. She became secretive, hiding her insecurity and fear, and as if withdrawing into a shell, or cocoon. Bern and I noticed this change but attributed the behavior (wrongly) to her obsessive will to achieve in her school work, to get all "A's," to win prizes. After all, she was bright and highly motivated and I thought she would mature and come closer once more. But this did not happen.

Jane was always high achieving, and obsessive about getting high marks. She was always on the Honor Roll. She was on the high school newspaper, wrote many articles. At graduation she won a DAR prize for citizenship. She was accepted at Wellesley College where she majored in history. She planned to go to Law School. During her Junior year she attended Princeton University, under a special exchange plan. She studied history and Chinese language. She returned to Wellesley to graduate, then to Harvard Law School. She ended up as Law Professor, Boston University Law School.

Her senior year at Wellesley she began an affair with Paul, her professor of History.

After graduation, Paul and his wife separated, then divorced. He received custody of their three small children (ages 5, 7, 9), and Jane and Paul were married. Our granddaughter Emily was born June 1970. Jane and Paul lived together with their four children until Emily was about 4–5 years old. Then suddenly, Jane took Emily and moved to Cambridge, separating from Paul and his children. We were never given an explanation, why she changed her mind so suddenly. No reason ever given why she uprooted Emily from her father and siblings. When she came home her senior year at Wellesley she told us that she wanted to marry Paul, who was married with three small children. We had numerous discussions with her, we went for counseling because we thought the situation was critical. She still had to go to Law School, and primarily we thought the most important reason to wait was that there were three small children involved. We could not see how she could undertake to be married, raise Paul's three children, and go to law school. We asked her to wait. We had no objection to her marrying Paul. We thought she understood that we were concerned for all of them. But, again, her obsession was to lead her.

Jane and Paul were divorced. When Emily was eleven, Jane married Larry, her second husband. Larry was a professor of Law at NYU. Now they are both Law Professors at University of Texas Law School. Emily has just completed the program for Acupuncture. She graduated with Massachusetts Certificate for practice of Acupuncture and Herbal Medicine.

Jonathan was born in 1948, a most beautiful child, round face like Bern, a butterball with deep set eye's like Bern. He was born after an easy quick delivery, smiling, always in good humor. He was a delightful little boy, a happy, smiling joyful little boy. And, he didn't walk, always skipping. He loved everyone, and everyone—grandparents, family. friends of our parents, and friends of ours smiled with him and loved him. He was a very affectionate child. He had a special love relationship with Max and Becky, an older couple, friends of our parents. They were another set of grandparents for him. They had a special affection for Jonathan. They lived close by and visited us daily, summer and winter to be with our children. They were family.

Jon was also the delight of all his teachers, all through school. He was bright, with a keen intellect, like Bern, and a happy, sparkling disposition. He had a sharp sense of humor (like Bern), very catching, always funny. His teachers loved his happy, exuberant personality, and his keen intellect. Of course he was highly motivated, like his parents, and a high achiever.

Until Jon was 17, a junior in high school, he was a well adjusted, happy young man, very handsome. In the early years he did not show any effects of the shock and trauma of living in the midst of the McCarthy panic terror and fear. Or any of the emotional fear we went through when Bern was uprooted from hjs job at Ft. Monmouth during the Army-McCarthy Hearings, with the terrible insecurity and fear that followed. He seemed to go about his business of achieving in school. In Spring of his junior year he came home one day with his head shaven. Bern and I were startled, but he had no explanation except to laugh. He said he did it for a "joke", and he decided that he could not be a 'doctor'. Whatever emotions he was internalizing he was not sharing with us. He was reading voraciously and continuously writing.

Jonathan graduated from high school with honors and went on to Wesleyan University. After a year he decided to transfer to Marlboro College, Vermont. He was not clear about his major interest, or career. After Marlboro, he continued writing and attended Columbia University School of Journalism, and earned a Master's degree. His professor said that Jon was exceptionally talented, and he was offered a teaching position. He taught at the Columbia School of Journalism for two years, then left to go to South America as a free-lance journalist. This was early 70's the time of the democratic election of Salvadore Allende in Chile. Jon was in Chile along with dozens of other young journalists, in 1973, when the democratically elected Allende was overthrown, and murdered, in a coup, sponsored by the CIA. The junta then installed Pinochet as president, one of the worst dictators of this century. Jonathan was lucky in escaping from Chile, along with most of the young journalists.

For the next ten years he wrote and published several books, one outstanding about the political situation in a Central American country. He traveled to Russia to write about a special ancient breed of horses and he made a documentary film about them. He now works as Assistant Editor of a large daily newspaper in West Paterson, New Jersey. He writes a weekly column for the paper.

After he returned from Chile he met a very fine woman, Sara, an editor at Rolling Stones Magazine. She was a warm friendly, bright and talented woman. They were married in Mexico. Although her office was in NYC, she moved in with Jon in the old house he had bought in Dennisville, NJ. (Cape May County) Sara became pregnant but at the same time she discovered a lump in her breast. With the help of the doctors at Sloan Kettering Hospital, (NYC) it was excised. But, the fetus had to be removed. Happily, Sara survived the surgery for breast cancer. It was the end of pregnancy.

It was also the end of the marriage. During the entire time of her illness, with two pregnancies and breast cancer Jonathan was not supportive, he did not behave in a caring manner. Instead, he was argumentative. He argued about every procedure that was recommended by Sara's doctors. This made the decisions more difficult for Sara. Also, at this time he was teaching a course at Louisiana State University, part time, and was away from home. We did not know until after their marriage broke up that he was involved with another woman there. He was having an affair with a woman who was divorced, and had a young child.

The marriage ended bitterly, although they seemed to remain friends. Sara did not want to end the marriage. It was Jon who was very disturbed, blaming her for everything. We suggested that he go for counseling. He went. He said that the psychologist "agreed with me, it was her fault." There was no mention of his instant temper tantrums, no explanation.

Sometime later, he communicated with Bern that he met a woman on the subway in NYC, She was a Russian immigrant. She was married to a Russian they had a young son. She had come to the US with her entire family, in the 70's along with a huge wave of Russian immigrants. Along with many other Russian émigrés they were settled in Coney Island (Brooklyn, N.Y.) where there was a large Russian immigrant population.

Jon wrote to Bern that he found the "perfect" woman, Lilia. He believed that Russian culture made women more submissive, and therefore less argumentative. She obtained a divorce, but retained custody of her son. They came to live with Jon in Dennisville, N.J.

Both our children lived with us through the intensely repressive period of McCarthyism in 1954 at Ft. Monmouth, through the period of Bern's loss of job and security. They were young, five and eight when this happened. our family life had been one of love and security for them. They seemed to be able to accommodate in the early years to the effect of these events and the trauma created in our lives. As each in their own way internalized the fear and paranoia that continued to haunt us. Each one was able to achieve in school, in career but it was in their personal relationship with us, that things fell apart. The long term effects of the lingering fear and insecurity, and paranoia had its effects on our personal relationships. For the next four decades we were alienated and our relationship was broken.

From Many Are The Crimes, by Ellen Schrecker: "The McCarthy Era was a bad time for freedom in America encompassing far more than the brief career of Senator Joseph McCarthy, it was the most widespread episode of political repression in the history of the United States." In the name of national security, most Americans supported the anti-communist crusade that ruined so many careers, marriages and even lives. Thousands of teachers, civil servants, union leaders, housewives and others were put on trial, lost their jobs, or ended up on blacklists. Its long-term effect was a submissive public.

WHAT HAPPENED TO OUR BRIGHT, BEAUTIFUL CHILDREN?

It is not unusual for two children raised in the same family, the same cultural landscape, the same emotional environment to have different personalities. And so it is not unusual for two children of the same family experiencing the same historical and political events of political repression and the trauma of terror and fear to internalize these painful events differently. Even though they have many similar characteristics. Jane and Jon were bright, gifted and talented, inheriting these talents from us. Both were keenly intelligent and strongly motivated and high achieving. Both were intellectually focused. But, the long term effect of the trauma and lingering fear which we experienced in the crucible of McCarthyism had different effects on their personalities and behavior.

In Jane's case: She was a highly sensitive child, with a sense of insecurity. She always needed additional attention, and praise. It is the case that the traumatic fear we experienced as a family in the McCarthy witch hunt, with the effect of fear and lingering paranoia on Bern, had a profound effect on her. That the only way she could cope with this excessive emotional strain was to withdraw into her private shell, her "own reality", as the psychologist said. This was the only way that she could continue to be high achieving, and achieve a career in law. Unfortunately, she was not aware that her withdrawal would disrupt our relationship, and cause us such long term grief and despair. The sad effect has been that it is most difficult for Jane to show affection and love, to touch, to hug, to express words of love.

Jonathan's case: In Jon's case, he seems to have internalized our terrible experience in the heart of the McCarthy witch hunts, but he has had no lessening of ties with us. As he grows older he is more able to control his outbursts, and to be his own humorous self. He easily shows his love and caring in our relationship. If Bern were here I am sure he would hold him and tell him how much he loved him

Our world, our children's world of happiness, love and devotion, was transformed by the climate of terror, panic and fear that was initiated in the McCarthy period. We were all suffering from the lingering fear, the trauma, the insecurity, the effect of the terribleness of history., the heart of darkness. In this rank atmosphere each one experienced their own personal nightmare, their own tragedy.

9

EPILOGUE: LINGERING FEAR: LIVING IN THE CRUCIBLE OF MCCARTHYISM; THE CENTER WOULD NOT HOLD

"It doesn't end, never will it end." (Gunter Grass)

"We must not only seek but find an alternative, because the world offered to us is unbearable. For years simply to seek a new world has been either a crime or a folly. From now on, it is the main item on the agenda." (Daniel Singer)

I started this memoir quoting the Mayan woman Petronila who said, "I want it to be remembered that this happened. We have to do everything to make sure that this never happens again."

My story is of an unbearable world in the era of the Cold War whipped up by terror and fear of McCarthyism. It is a narrative of tragic realism. My story illustrates the lasting damage to our family as a result. To make sure that this never happens again a new world is not only desirable but necessary.

The question of what to do with our memories goes to the very heart of my story. Not a day goes by that I do not go over in my mind, during the day and night, the events that took place during the McCarthy witch hunt in that time so long ago. And how the effects of the initial trauma and fear was later revealed in the damage to our children and their relationship with us. How this damaged or destroyed our family's loving relationship. How our children revealed what they were feeling. Often it was just a look, a facial expression. Sometimes it was only a slight remark. It was as if they were only showing signals, like a yellow traffic light noting caution. But it was enough to tell us that they felt distanced. They were protecting themselves. They were still feeling the fear.

It is not just a narrative history of our family over four generations. It is a memoir of tragic realism of the long term damaging effects on our family in the McCarthy witch hunt campaign of fear and terror.

I can only repeat what the Mayan woman Petronila said: I want "to make sure that we do everything we can that this never happens again". What I do with these memories goes to the heart of the society. What kind of society, what kind of culture do we want? What kind of life do we want for our children and grandchildren?

Bern and I grew up during the Depression years when jobs and a living wage were the life line to a good life. This was the time of the democratic ideal in American life. Like most young people of that time, the 30's and 40's, we had achieved a higher education. We went to college. It was a time for getting a job and pursuing a career. To Bern, he thought of a career job that would pay a living wage and provide security for the future. We knew from the experience of our parents, what it meant to have a job without security, to be suddenly thrown out of work, unable to support a family. Bern felt that the need for security was the most important part of the job.

That is why, just after his graduation with an MS in engineering, he took the Civil Service exams. He passed with a perfect score and got a job with the Civil Service Commission in N.Y.C. After his Navy service he was transferred to the job at Ft. Monmouth. He knew that he had a good job with living wage to support his family, and with security. He was the happiest of men.

As I look back at those years, all alone, we were such a happy family, secure in our love and devotion with two beautiful children, and with Bern in a job he loved. I think of the metaphor of trying to survive in a churning sea, being pulled down by the current of political machinations of the McCarthy storm. It was a total disruption of the democratic ideal of the American life.

The 50's was an ugly era in American history. It was the time just after World War II under the Truman Administration and the fearful crusade against communism, and the Red Scare. It was a decisive time of American foreign policy. It was the beginning of the Cold War policies, how the policies were shaped through the following decades until today. The events set in motion by the Truman Administration would eventually shape this country's course into the present.

One of the most sinister aspects examined by historians was the penchant for governing by what Richard Freeland called "crisis politics". That is when the president and his chief advisors find it more convenient to make decisions without the knowledge of the electorate. But instead, with deceit and manipulation using "baseless claims of impending danger" to our security. All with intent to create a climate of fear. The era, the landscape, the climate is the same now. We have skipped over two generations and returned to the same use of "crisis politics" of war scare and fear.

Another world is necessary. We are living in a time labeled "New World Order" (by Bush I), which has seen declining economies, growing inequality, and marked by pre-emptive wars. All inside a system which has failed to meet human needs. As expressed by David Nelly in Another World Is Possible "We must strive to understand the system as it is a system that organizes our lives and the political and social strategies we need to change it."

September 11 began the first day of a new McCarthy era. Once again we find ourselves living in a landscape of global war. The rhetoric focuses on nation security and sacrifice. The administration has again created a climate of fear in order to frighten the people for purposes of their own. The war in Iraq is the first example.

A story out of Wisconsin illustrates the climate of fear and the suppression of liberties.

The King (George Bush) made a visit to Wisconsin, a bus trip across western Wisconsin. As is typical when monarchs travel, the schools and roads were closed preventing residents from moving about freely. But the people in western Wisconsin still hold onto the idea that they live in a free republic. "There is a pattern of harassment of free speech here that really concerns me." Says Guy Wolf, the student services coordinator at the Univ. of Wisconsin, La Crosse. The residents felt that their free speech was curtailed.

Along the route of the Bush bus trip, the Bush team created a "no-free speech zone" that excluded any expression of dissent, which is, as we know, the life-blood of democracy. Two citizens holding up signs that criticized the president were arrested. One was slapped with a disorderly conduct ticket. Further on, up the road, in La Crosse, the clampdown on civil liberties was even more sweeping. Hundreds of citizens were told that they could not make noise or display certain signs. They were forced to stand out of sight. None could understand why they had to give up their free speech rights, normally protected by the First Amendment to the Constitution. The Bush visit had attacked their First Amendment rights.

This narrative is of our family caught in the tragic events of the era of the Cold War and the McCarthy witch hunts and the climate of terror. Joseph Conrad understood that the distinctions between civilized London and "the heart of darkness" quickly collapsed in extreme situations, and that the heights of European civilization could instantly fall into the most barbarous practices against its own citizens. Conrad described the use of terrorism in its most vicious attacks and its most barbarous use. Those times have been repeated and repeated, and again today.

In our case, we were swept away in the flood of events of McCarthyism. In retrospect it is as if our lives were worthless, insignificant in the scheme of national politics. We were what is called "collateral damage' in the trumped up hunt for "communists and spies" among government employees. But, no historian or academic has chronicled the damage, the long term effect of witch hunts on the families of the engineers caught in the McCarthy web. No one has recorded how many innocent families were attacked or, how the psychological fear instituted as McCarthyism left its mark on the children of these families. The experience of psychological fear and terror of McCarthy's witch hunt lies buried in our psyches. It has left its imprint on our family's dysfunctional relationships and derailed, disoriented love for each other.

The violence of historical events in our personal lives can transform a calm happy, almost lyrical landscape into a raging storm, leaving permanent damage.

James Baldwin said, "The great force of our history is that we carry it within us, and that we are unconsciously controlled by it in many ways."

Arthur Miller said that past events and present realities have always been pressed together by a moral logic. In his play, The Crucible, 1953, about the Salem Witch Trials, in 1682, those presumed to be witches were hanged. The presumptions were little more than fantasies conjured by a mixture of fear, frustration, jealousy and pride. In 1957, the Massachusetts General Court passed a resolution declaring the proceedings to be "the result of popular hysterical fear of the Devil." The earlier laws had been superceded by laws "more civilized." It had taken 300 years for the state to acknowledge its responsibility for those who died in the trumped up trials.

In our case, and in the large number of cases of personal and family damage as a result of the McCarthy witch hunts no responsibility was ever taken. The Administration never acknowledged that the McCarthy witch hunts/or inquisitions, and the Red baiting and branding people as unpatriotic, as in the case of The Hollywood Ten, was in order to create a climate of fear and terror. Thus allowing the Truman administration to carry on the military build up of the Cold War. Now, in the year 2000, the similar climate of fear, and scare tactics are being instituted, for the very same reasons.

The story of the Salem Witch Trials is also portrayed by author Marion Starkey. It is said to be in "classic dramatic form", Starkey insisted "Here is real Greek tragedy. It is human reality with tragic results for the few. The story of 1692 is really an allegory of our times…The question is not the reality of witches but the power of authority to define the nature of the real."

Miller said, of the early fifties, "We were all going slightly crazy trying to be honest and trying to see straight and trying to be safe.' "It seemed to me that the atmosphere of hysteria in Salem had a certain inner procedure, which we were duplicating once again. And that by revealing the nature of that procedure some light could be thrown on what we were doing to ourselves."

"Today, not only do accused witches still die, in more than one country in the world, but groundless accusations are still granted credence, hysteria still claims its victims, persecution still masquerades as virtue, and prejudice as piety. Nor has the need to resist coercive myths or to assert moral truths passed with such a final act of absolution. The witch finder is ever vigilant. No one would challenge his authority?"

These final words of Arthur Miller sum up the intense belief that this story, a memoir of human suffering, which resembles that of a true Greek tragedy, must be read and remembered by large numbers of the American public. It is a reiteration of the question of "power of the authority to define the nature of the real."

This is our story, a narrative of human reality with tragic results. With this memoir I hope to make an impact on the American consciousness: That this never be allowed to happen again in this country.

McCarthyism changed the lives of thousands of people at the same time that it changed the nation's political culture. It also shaped our society.

Much of the damage that McCarthyism imposed was psychological. (Some of the federal employees could not deal with the "trauma of having been accused by their own government of being disloyal to their country." "The situation was most disorienting for those who had no connection with the left." (Schrecker)

And then there was the fear. The fear and paranoia were pervasive. "With loyalty security panels questioning federal workers about their reading habits…Children did not escape the anxiety, the fear, and the paranoia of their parents."

The greatest damage of McCarthyism was to our rights of Free Speech under the First Amendment. Our Civil Rights, under the Bill of Rights, and our political freedom. McCarthyism created a legacy. It showed how effectively political repression could operate within a democratic society. It showed the willingness of many politicians and leaders to subscribe to a demonized view of the world and to limit political debate in the name of national security. The process deformed American politics, it made possible the blatant disregard for the rights of the individual. It legitimized a police state (under J. Edgar Hoover.) During the McCarthy era, The First Amendment was nullified.

McCarthyism contributed to the undermining of respect for lawful procedures at the highest levels of government, and to a sleaziness in American politics. And it is still happening today. The demonizing of marginalized groups and the use of state power to suppress them goes on all the time. Only now it is happening with a special vigor under Attorney General John Ashcroft, who is ready to overthrow all our rights, our civil liberties, and political freedom as well.

We must not let this happen again. We must do everything we can to see that it does not happen again.

McCarthyism Redux: The relevance, the timeliness of current events.
"The future of repression looks frighteningly bright. The Patriot act is a major step in removing constitutional protections of privacy, trial by jury, and indirectly the rights of free speech and assembly. And of permitting the use of federal troops against the civilian population, and of allowing the selective suspension of habeas corpus protection…Of course, denial of our Constitutional rights of free speech and assembly is becoming better organized, better armed, and more ruthless." "The Bush administration is advancing the repression agenda as fast as is feasible, i.e. the Patriot Act II." (Edward Herman, Z Magazine)

Some methods of violence may target and destroy the lives of the innocent victims. A society bingeing on fear—is vulnerable, to destruction, like a nostalgic echo of the Cold War it is using fear to advance a different, more repressive agenda. It is contrary to an open and free society.
The government already had a "no-fly list", a "shipper's list", a new "Computer Assisted Profile "system for "mining data". Only a few of the many Kafkaesque technological methods the government is designing. It is a huge web network to catch innocent civilians, to destroy their lives under the rubric of security. We have a new order organized around fear. Are we on the way to the new wave of McCarthyism with control of the American people by terror and fear?
We must find another way. We must not live in the heart of darkness.
The tapestry of our lives is the metaphor of fear. Our loving relationship bashed against the rocks by the sea of McCarthyism, love vanished in the waves of the heart.

The End

978-0-595-37328-4
0-595-37328-3

Printed in the United States
45909LVS00006B/256-321